PRAYERS FOR THE SEASONS OF GOD'S PEOPLE

Worship Aids for the Revised Common Lectionary, Year B

B. David Hostetter

ABINGDON PRESS
Nashville

PRAYERS FOR THE SEASONS OF GOD'S PEOPLE:
WORSHIP AIDS FOR THE REVISED COMMON LECTIONARY, YEAR B

Copyright © 1999 by Abingdon Press

This book is printed on acid-free, recycled paper.

Library of Congress Cataloging-in-Publication Data

Hostetter, B. David, 1926–
    Prayers for the seasons of God's people: Worship aids for the
Revised common lectionary, Year B/B. David Hostetter.
        p.   cm.
    ISBN 0-687-33664-3 (alk. paper)
    1. Common lectionary (1992).   2. Pastoral prayers.   3. Litanies.
I. Title.
BV30.H65   1998
264'.13—dc21
                                                                    98-52205
                                                                         CIP

Scripture quotations, unless otherwise indicated, are from the New Revised Standard Version Bible, copyright © 1989, by the Division of Christian Education of the National Council of the Churches of Christ in the United States of America.

99 00 01 02 03 04 05 06 07 08—10 9 8 7 6 5 4 3 2 1

MANUFACTURED IN THE UNITED STATES OF AMERICA

Contents

After Pentecost

Preface

As I prepare the text for this publication I am aware of my indebtedness to many others whose prayers and books of prayers have been my inspiration over the years. In addition to the acknowledgment at the beginning of the volumes for years C and A, I want to mention also The Rev. William Barclay, with whom I had personal correspondence regarding his Prayers for Help and Healing.

I often used his prayers that were published in the British Weekly and followed his lead when leaving the old "Thees and Thous" to "You and Yours." The prayers here will re-echo his and others' phrases.

B. David Hostetter

Advent/Christmas

First Sunday of Advent

First Lesson - The prophet urges God to make a dramatic entrance into the world and impress the nations. Isaiah 64:1-9

Psalm 80:1-7, 17-19

Second Lesson - This is the beginning of Paul's first letter to the church at Corinth. 1 Corinthians 1:3-9

Gospel - Jesus alerts the disciples in apocalyptic terms of the coming of the Son of Man in clouds of glory. Mark 13:24-37

CALL TO WORSHIP

Pastor: The grace of our Lord Jesus Christ be with you all.

People: And also with you.

Pastor: Wait expectantly for our Lord Jesus Christ to reveal himself. He will keep you firm to the end, without reproach on the Day of our Lord Jesus.

People: It is God in Person, who called us to share in the life of the Son, Jesus Christ our Lord; and God keeps faith.

INVOCATION

Eternal God, we wait upon you at this time, alerting ourselves to watch also for the currents of history, the rivers of time that roll on, generation after generation. We come especially to give thanks that your Son Jesus came among us to share our life so that we might share yours. Your Spirit inspires our prayers in the name of Jesus, our Savior. Amen

PRAYER OF CONFESSION

God of many names, by what name shall we call to you? Our question rises out of some confusion, not only about who you are, but about who we are, for you have declared yourself to be our kin, One who has ransomed us. In some ways you are like a permissive parent, who allows us enough room to get ourselves into trouble when we follow undisciplined instincts. Too often we are more like people who claim no affinity to you than like a people who bear your name. Forgive our tendency to slough off responsibility for our decision. Excuse the incompleteness of many of our confessions. We trust you still because of Jesus Christ, your Son. Amen

Declaration of Pardon

Pastor: Friends, hear the good news! God has given you grace and peace in Christ Jesus

People: and enriched us with many good gifts.

Pastor: Friends, believe the good news!

People: In Jesus Christ, we are forgiven.

[AND]

Exhortation

Be alert and watchful, for no one knows when the Son of Man will come with great power and glory. Do not neglect to finish the work he has given you to do.

PRAYER OF THE DAY

Divine Timekeeper, keep us alert by the chimes of the times that whether Christ comes again, at dawn or high noon, in the evening or at midnight, we will be ready to welcome his return, enabled by the Spirit to show that our house is in order and that we are honored by his coming. Amen

PRAYER OF THANKSGIVING

God of grace, Child of peace, Spirit of truth, we join with all the members of the church everywhere in the world in giving thanks for all the gifts you have given to enrich the whole church. Though each of us does not have all gifts, there is no needful gift lacking to your church through the talents you have distributed among us. In Jesus Christ you have given us life and truth, grace and peace. Through days of persecution and days of plenty, you have sustained the church and kept it firm in expectation of the return of the Lord, Jesus Christ. Your favor is unmerited. Your peace is undeserved. Your truth is beyond our comprehension. We celebrate your generosity, in Jesus Christ. Amen

PRAYER OF DEDICATION

1999

Lord of the church, you are not enriched by our gifts but enable us to share our talents for the enrichment of the whole congregation, young and old and middle aged. We present ourselves to be useful to each other and to you. Amen

PRAYERS OF INTERCESSION
AND COMMEMORATION

1999

God of the ages, from ages past no one has heard, no ear has perceived, no eye has seen anyone besides you, who works for those who wait for him. You meet those who gladly do right, those who remember you in your ways. You are concerned not only about us in our own neighborhood but all the nations of the world and every locale. Though you are the Creator who may destroy what you have made like a potter with a pot that is imperfect, you reshape human societies in expectation of a more perfect vessel. Continue to speak to the nations through the scriptures and the church that there may be a new heaven and new earth redeemed from rebellion and violence.

As we approach another Christmas and listen for the angelic anthem of peace on earth, grant the world not only the traditional "cease fires" that often suspend armed conflict at the season but a spirit of reconciliation that should be the approach of the church of Christ. May the church in every nation preach the apostolic message: "Grace to you and peace from God our Father and the Lord Jesus Christ . . ."

Strengthen and purify the church so that it may be blameless on the day of our Lord Jesus Christ.

By your power, great God, our Lord Jesus healed the sick, giving new hope to the hopeless. Though we cannot command or possess your power, we pray for those who want to be healed. Close wounds, cure sickness, make the broken whole again, so that the ill may be well and happy in newness of life. Help us to welcome every healing as a sign that, though death is against us, you are for us, and have promised renewed and risen life in Jesus Christ the Lord.

In the coming of Jesus of Nazareth, Invisible God, you have let your face shine on us so that we may be saved. We rejoice in the salvation of all who from the beginning have put their trust in your grace and been received into glory. Enrich us in the testimony of Christ so that we are not lacking in any spiritual gift as we wait for the new revealing of our Lord Jesus Christ or in death we are taken to be with him. To our Lord Jesus, to our faithful God, to your ever present Holy Spirit, we ascribe all grace and peace, time without end. Amen

Second Sunday of Advent

First Lesson - The prophet advocates smoothing the way for the coming of God like a just and caring Shepherd. Isaiah 40:1-11

Psalm 85:1-2, 8-13

Second Lesson - Peter reaffirms the declaration of Jesus that the time of the second coming is a surprise but that the upheaval will bring justice and peace. 2 Peter 3:8-15*a*

Gospel - The beginning of Mark's Gospel connects the ministry of Jesus with the prophecy of Isaiah and identifies John the Baptist as the forerunner of Jesus Christ. Mark 1:1-8

CALL TO WORSHIP

Pastor: The grace of our Lord Jesus Christ be with you all.

People: And also with you.

Pastor: Hear the words of the Lord. Are they not words of peace, peace to God's people?

People: We hear the words of our Lord Jesus to us, his loyal servants, and to all who turn and trust in him.

INVOCATION

Holy God, we come to worship you, to confess that we believe you to be just and merciful. You send us the Prince of Peace to lead us in paths of peace. Lead us by your Spirit that we may follow him always. Amen

PRAYER OF CONFESSION

God of the first day, God of today, God of the last day, we admit that we are more frightened by the threat of a nuclear accident or a nuclear war than we are hopeful for a new heaven and earth. It is like our apprehension of major surgery, an unpleasant experience, but one that can bring about the condition in which healing can take place. We may be fatalistic and feel powerless to change unjust institutions that provoke and promote war. Forgive our reluctance to look for the new day and to work for justice and peace with patience, repentance, and perseverance, whatever the disappointments and delays. Baptize us with the

Holy Spirit according to the gospel of Jesus Christ, your Son. Amen

Declaration of Pardon

Pastor: Friends, hear the good news! God has forgiven your guilt

People: and put away all our sins.

Pastor: Friends, believe the good news!

People: In Jesus Christ, we are forgiven.

[AND]

Exhortation

Prepare a road for the Lord through the barren places of our common life. Clear a highway for God across the fruitless areas of our history.

PRAYER OF THE DAY

Jesus Christ, Son of God, since you have walked in our shoes, enable us by the same Holy Spirit of our baptism to proclaim the good news and prepare the way for your coming again so that you may be surrounded by people from all earth's cities and countrysides. Amen

PRAYER OF THANKSGIVING

Saving God, loving Christ, baptizing Spirit, hear our thanksgiving for all who have paved the way for your good news to reach us. We admire the bold preaching of the prophets and apostles. We appreciate the work of scholars and translators in preparing a written text for us to read. We are grateful for the printers and binders who make Bibles for us and for all who help us to read and understand the Word of God written. Most of all we thank you that your saving and forgiving love was embodied in Jesus of Nazareth, the great Good Shepherd who has gathered his flock into the church. For past deliverance, for present comfort, for future promise we give you thanks, faithful God. Amen

PRAYER OF DEDICATION

We worship you, loving and faithful Lord, by the presentation of these tokens of our prosperity and the yield of our work. Use us and our offerings to spread the gospel of Jesus Christ. Amen

PRAYERS OF INTERCESSION AND COMMEMORATION

Comfort your people, O God, not only in Jerusalem, torn with racial and religious tensions, but inner cities of the world so often the scene of poverty and prostitution, and violence against persons and property.

Sustain the voices of repentance and new life in the inner city and in every moral wilderness, to prepare the way of the Lord and help the lost to find a highway to God and a better life. Reveal the glory of the Christ Child again in the rough places of human pain and poverty.

While the church waits for the second coming of Christ and a new heaven and earth, may we strive to be found by him at peace, without spot or blemish; and using the time of your patience to preach the good news of salvation by word and work.

Faithful God: you have power to set us free from harmful habits and addictions. May those who are hooked on drugs and addictions too strong to control be given healing help that they may recover and be free again. Keep us from condemning the addictions of others and overlooking our own ungoverned passions. Enable us to be examples of serenity and self-control to the praise of the name of Jesus Christ.

O God, before you the generations rise and pass away. You are the strength of those who labor; you are the rest of the blessed dead. We rejoice in the company of your saints.

We remember all who have lived in faith, all who have peacefully died, and especially those dear to us who rest in you. Give us in time our portion with those who have trusted in you and have striven to do your holy will. To your name, with the church on earth and the church in heaven, we ascribe all honor and glory, now and forever. Amen

Third Sunday of Advent

First Lesson - The prophet brings glad tidings of relief and renewal. Isaiah 61:1-4, 8-11

Psalm 126

Second Lesson - Paul urges cautious optimism as Christians give thanks and pray while waiting for the second coming of Christ. 1 Thessalonians 5:16-24

Gospel - John the Baptist, though a lesser light, is a light widening the eyes of people to see the brighter light of the Christ. John 1:6-8, 19-28

CALL TO WORSHIP

Pastor: The grace of our Lord Jesus Christ be with you all.

People: And also with you.

Pastor: Tell out the greatness of the Lord.

People: We will rejoice in God our Savior.

INVOCATION

Saving God, with joy we come to worship you and proclaim by our presence and by our attention that we are grateful for your many mercies to us and to all. You are worthy to be praised for the majesty of your creation and the grace of our Lord Jesus Christ. How great you are! Amen

PRAYER OF CONFESSION

Infinite Parent, Incarnate Offspring, Inclusive Spirit, in Jesus Christ you have experienced our humanity. We admit that we are not yet holy in spirit, soul, and body. Our worship is not always wholehearted. Our hearts and minds are often arrogant, prejudiced, unchangeable. Our bodies are too prone to rule us, and bad habits jeopardize our health. Forgive our faults and fulfill your promise through the communion of the Holy Spirit that we may be faultless when our Lord Jesus comes, to the glory of your great name. Amen

Declaration of Pardon

Pastor: Friends, hear the good news! God's mercy is sure from generation to generation, and firm in the promise to our ancestors.

People: God will not forget to show mercy to their children's children.

Pastor: Friends, believe the good news!

People: In Jesus Christ, we are forgiven.

[AND]

Exhortation

Be always joyful. Pray continually. Give thanks whatever happens; for this is what God in Christ wills for you.

PRAYER OF THE DAY

Outgoing God, gift us again with the Holy Spirit that we may make way for you to the humble with good news, to the captives with promises of release, to the bereaved with the comfort of beauty and new gladness, to the broken-hearted with tender, loving care, and to the oppressed with the promise of eventual justice. Lord God, make righteousness and praise blossom before all nations. Amen

PRAYER OF THANKSGIVING

Hallowed be your name, mighty God, hallowed be your name, merciful God. Hallowed be your name, active God, you side with the humble rather than the proud, with the poor rather than the rich, with the powerless rather than the powerful. You come into our world in Mary's child, Jesus of Nazareth, the Son nearest your heart, full of grace and truth. Thanks be given to you always, in Hebrew and Greek and English and in every language of the universe. Amen

PRAYER OF DEDICATION

God, who promised to come, has come, and has promised to come again, we are preparing ourselves for your return and offer our gifts and ourselves to make the way straight for Jesus Christ our Lord. Amen

PRAYERS OF INTERCESSION AND COMMEMORATION

Creator God, continue your activity in the creation, maintaining and sustaining the forces that operate our galaxy in your universe, which you made and called good. Redeemer God, who has entered our sphere of life in Jesus of Nazareth, complete your saving work in our world, repairing the ravages of human disobedience and conflict so that peace may be more than a cessation of war, bombings, assassinations, plots and counterplots, and a perfect humanity finally be regained.

God of the prophets, inspire our young men and our

young women to dream dreams of genuine prosperity and progress and peace. When age and illness make us less productive, give us grace to make places for those capable of succeeding us and carrying on the best of what we have begun and adding to it new projects and services that will enrich our common life.

Timeless Father, Eternal Brother, Mothering Spirit: you have set the solitary in families and seek to teach us to love others as we love ourselves, honestly and graciously. May we be teachable in every generation from the oldest to the youngest knowing how great your wisdom is and how fallible we can be. Grant us the spirit of forgiveness that, confessing our faults to one another, we may forgive and be forgiven; through Jesus Christ our Savior.

God of past and future, dying and rising Savior, eternal and contemporary Spirit, hear our prayers for the people of your world, in which you live, but in which there are also powers of evil and of death. Overcome evil in and through us. Call the nations of the world to new experiments in cooperation so that all the gifts of the earth's people may be put to good use for the common good. Guide the leaders of both management and labor to new ways of achieving economic justice in the sharing of profit and in serving fairly the needs of consumers.

Give wisdom to all who seek to redefine the borderline between life and death, which the medical community has expanded in so many ways that it is difficult to know what prolongs dying and what prolongs genuine human life. Give wisdom to governments as to the responsibility of parents and what are the limits of government intervention in private decision-making by individuals and by parents for their minor children.

Bless and uphold all who live on the borderline between life and death and those who keep watch with them. May your love and grace be sufficient for all.

Give continuing wisdom and skill to all in the medical community who look for new ways of healing and helping us to live longer. Bless as well all who are involved in hospice and others also dedicated to helping us through the final valley of the shadow of death. May your grace, mercy, and peace be with the dying and sustain in hope those who die a little with them.

God of the living, we give thanks for the rest and peace of those you have taken to yourself. May we hear your gracious invitation above all other voices when the hour of our death comes. These and all our prayers we offer to you through Jesus Christ our Lord. Amen

Fourth Sunday of Advent

First Lesson - David is promised God's unfailing love and a long, disciplined dynasty to follow him on the throne. 2 Samuel 7:1-11, 16

Psalm 89:1-4, 19-26 or **Luke** 1:46b-55

Second Lesson - Paul's letter to the Romans is concluded with a dignified doxology. Romans 16:25-27

Gospel - The angel Gabriel announces to Mary that she is favored by God to be the mother of God's Son. Luke 1:26-38

CALL TO WORSHIP

Pastor: The grace of our Lord Jesus Christ be with you all.

People: And also with you.

Pastor: Happy are the people who have learned to give acclaim to God.

People: We walk in the light of the Lord's presence.

INVOCATION

God of light, in whom is no darkness, in our darkest days we come to you seeking enlightenment and the guidance of the Spirit as you speak to us through your Word, written and human in Jesus Christ, who has taught us to pray. Amen

PRAYER OF CONFESSION

God to humanity descending, man to God ascended, God to all condescending, you send prophets to lead adulterous royalty to repentance and angels to innocent, common folk to direct them in your service. Forgive any unwillingness we have shown to do your will, any reticence to proclaim the good news of Jesus Christ, any doubt that your promised kingdom will fully come and will not fail. We have not been prepared to serve you at the risk of personal reputation or at hazard of private wealth. Have mercy on us, for the sake of Jesus Christ, who served your purpose without reservation. Amen

Declaration of Pardon

Pastor: Friends, hear the good news! The Divine secret kept in silence for long ages has been disclosed through the proclamation of Jesus Christ.

People: The prophetic scriptures have made known to us and to all nations.

Pastor: Friends, believe the good news!

People: In Jesus Christ, we are forgiven.

[AND]

Exhortation

Come in faith and obedience to God through Jesus Christ that the presence of the Holy Spirit may make your standing sure, to the glory of God.

PRAYER OF THE DAY

God of all life, grant to us who are called to parenthood your Holy Spirit to develop our self-control, that in begetting and conceiving, we may give birth to holy children, dedicated to you by their baptism and nurtured in your service through our family life, by Jesus Christ, Son of the Most High. Amen

PRAYER OF THANKSGIVING

We will sing the story of your love, O God, forever. We will proclaim your faithfulness to all generations. You declare your true love in covenants made with humble nations. You reassure the lowly person of your gracious favor. You call young and old alike to serve your purposes and complete your loving designs. We celebrate the motherhood of young Mary and old Elizabeth. We mark again with great joy the birth of the Son of God, the son of David, the son of Mary, Jesus of Nazareth, known as Joseph's son. We worship you, God the sender. We worship you, Jesus, the sent One, Son of the most high and son of the most humble. We worship you, Holy Spirit, God in touch with our humanity. Glory be to God in heaven and earth. Amen

PRAYER OF DEDICATION

The most majestic music is not an adequate gift of adoration to you and yet you hear the simplest song. The most precious gift is beneath your notice and yet you receive whatever is given out of the deepest poverty. Let our gifts and our lives be worthy of you as they can be only in the grace of our Lord Jesus Christ and the enabling Spirit. Amen

PRAYERS OF INTERCESSION
AND COMMEMORATION

God of all, everywhere, hear our prayers this morning for all who at this season, when we especially like to be with family and friends, are separated from them. Grant that visits and gifts to those who are in hospitals or nursing homes or prisons may be the means of making your love more real to them.

Bless those who are busy in emergency services: those whose own safety is in jeopardy as they seek survivors of disasters, those who bring food and emergency treatment to the fire victims, those who are on call in ambulance, fire, and police services.

Bless families who are separated by divorce or difficulty that the spirit of the season may mellow differences and bring comfort and accommodation especially for the sake of children.

Heal the sick, comfort the dying and the bereaved. May the good news of your advent in the birth of the Christ Child renew the faith of the doubting who may feel unloved and abandoned by you as by others.

Grant guidance and correction to the leaders of the nations that there may be continued negotiations between governments and allies that may diminish threats of conflict and make real the song of peace on earth, goodwill to humanity.

God of all times and places, we praise you for all your servants who, having been faithful to you on earth, now live with you in heaven. Keep us in communion with them until we meet with all your children in the joy of your eternal kingdom; through Jesus Christ our Lord. Amen

Christmas Eve/Day
(First Proper A, B, C)

First Lesson - In the darkness the prophet welcomes the light of the great king in the line of David who will bring justice and peace. Isaiah 9:2-7

Psalm 96

Second Lesson - The grace of God that was made personal in Jesus Christ is expected again. Titus 2:11-14

Gospel - In Bethlehem, a shepherd's town, is born the Savior who is Mary's little Jesus, a descendant of the great king, David. Luke 2:1-14, (15-20)

CALL TO WORSHIP

Pastor: The grace of our Lord Jesus Christ be with you all.

People: And also with you.

Pastor: Silence, everyone, in the presence of God.

People: God has come out of the sanctuary of heaven.

INVOCATION

God of mystery, God of revelation, God of joyful sound, we worship you with the most profound devotion, and with the simplest wonder at the foot of a manger bed, singing in the Spirit so that our joy may be received as true worship; in the name of Jesus Christ. Amen

PRAYER OF CONFESSION

God of all worlds, ours seems at times like an abandoned one. We share in its sin, its darkness, and its despair. We

24

feel that you have left us alone to find our own way out of the mess we have made of things. We have forgotten that the world was created by you, revisited by you in Jesus Christ, and is still yours, a dwelling place of your choice for your Spirit. Forgive the belief that you are nowhere, that forgets that you are now here, in the Spirit of Jesus Christ. Amen

Declaration of Pardon

Pastor: Friends, hear the good news! The Lord has come, and is coming again.

People: May the peace of God keep guard over our hearts and our thoughts in Christ Jesus.

Pastor: Friends, believe the good news!

People: In Jesus Christ, we are forgiven.

[AND]

Exhortation

The Lord is near. Have no anxiety, but in everything make your requests known to God in prayer and petition with thanksgiving.

PRAYER OF THE DAY

Child of Bethlehem, Man of Nazareth, Christ of God, with Mary we treasure the stories of your birth and ponder over these things. May the celebration of your birth, both in this place and in our social circles, bring glory and praise to your name. Amen

PRAYER OF THANKSGIVING

Shepherd of Israel, Lamb of God, Keeper of Christ's flock, with Bethlehem shepherds of old, we come to see what has happened and consider what has been made known to us. We rejoice in the birth of this child Jesus who embodies both the Good Shepherd and the Lamb of God that takes away the sin of the world. For his obedience to your saving purpose we are thankful. That you become involved in the sin and suffering of our world, we are astonished. That you continue to draw us together as your flock by the Spirit we are comforted. Amen

PRAYER OF DEDICATION

Not often enough, O God, do we offer you the gift of our silence, in adoration, in attentiveness, in anticipation of your directions. Receive us in this solemn moment, and in such times of silence as we find for you in the days to come. Amen

PRAYERS OF INTERCESSION
AND COMMEMORATION

Almighty and ever-living God, by your apostle you taught us to pray not only for ourselves but for others, and to give thanks for all of life.

Heavenly Parent of all Fathers and Mothers and Families: guard the laughter of children and their playfulness. Bring them safely through injury and illness, so they may live the promises you give. Do not let us be so preoccupied with our work that we fail to hear their voices, or pay attention to them and their special vision of truth; but keep us with them, ready to listen and to love, even as in Jesus Christ you have loved us, your grown-up, sometimes wayward children.

First Creator: by your love we are given children through the miracle of birth. May we greet each new child with joy and surround them with faith so they may know who you are and want to be disciples of Jesus Christ. Remind us never to neglect our children either physically or spiritually but show them the loving acceptance that was the model given us by Joseph and Mary and by Jesus himself.

Inspire your whole church with the spirit of power, unity, and peace. Grant that all who trust you may receive your Word, and live together in love.

Lead all nations in the way of justice and goodwill. Direct those who govern, that they may rule fairly, maintain order, uphold those in need, and defend oppressed people; that this world may claim your rule and know true peace.

Give grace to all who proclaim the gospel through Word and Sacrament and deeds of mercy, that by their teaching and example they may bring others into your communion.

Comfort and relieve, O God, all who are in trouble, sorrow, poverty, sickness, grief, or any other need, especially those known to us whom we name before you in silence. Heal them in body, mind, or circumstance, working in them, by your grace, wonders beyond all they may dream or hope.

Eternal God, we remember before you those who have lived with us who have directed our steps in the Way, opened our eyes to the truth, inspired our hearts by their witness, and strengthened our wills by their devotion. We rejoice in their lives dedicated to your service. We honor them in their death, and pray that we may be united with them in the glory of Christ's resurrection. Amen

First Sunday After Christmas Day

First Lesson - Zion is as joyful as a bride when God clothes her with the garments of salvation. Isaiah 61:10–62:3

Psalm 148

Second Lesson - In Paul's letter to the Galatians he speaks of the timely birth of God's Son, our Savior. Galatians 4:4-7

Gospel - Joseph and Mary have the correct religious rituals for baby Jesus and themselves. Luke 2:22-40

CALL TO WORSHIP

Pastor: The grace of our Lord Jesus Christ be with you all.

People: And also with you.

Pastor: Let us rejoice in God with all our hearts.

People: Our Savior robes us with salvation like a garment and clothes us in integrity like a cloak.

INVOCATION

Eternal Parent, whatever the festive clothes we wear to mark this Christmas season, continue to receive us as robed with the white robes of salvation and wrapped in the cloak of your Spirit's integrity. Your Son Jesus is worthy of all adoration and praise. We bow down before him. Amen

PRAYER OF CONFESSION

Spirit of God, given to guide us to the place of prayer and to open our minds and hearts to what we should know, we confess that we do not always heed your bidding and often miss seeing what you have shown to those who have been obedient to your prompting. Forgive the stubbornness that resists learning, not admitting our need to know or confessing the sins we seek to hide. Amen

Declaration of Pardon

Pastor: Friends, hear the good news! God sent his own Son, born of a woman, born under the law, to purchase freedom for the slaves of the law.

People: Now we have the dignity of God's heirs with Jesus Christ.

Pastor: Friends, believe the good news!

People: In Jesus Christ, we are forgiven.

[AND]

Exhortation

As God's children, grow in wisdom and stature and in favor with God and your neighbors.

PRAYER OF THE DAY

Eternal Spirit, so guide us in worship and in learning that we may experience your salvation and speak with confidence of your grace through Jesus Christ. Amen

PRAYER OF THANKSGIVING

Eternal God, historic Christ, timeless Spirit, we rejoice in the salvation that you have planned and are fulfilling in the birth of Christ Jesus and in the continuing work of the Spirit in the church. You have freed us who have believed and are liberating those who are coming to faith in Jesus Christ. You bring goodness and beauty to flower in neighborhoods and nations. All praise be given to you, O God. Amen

PRAYER OF DEDICATION

As in their poverty the holy family brought their simple offerings to the temple, O God, so we bring our offerings in thanksgiving for the salvation you have brought us through Jesus Christ, your Son, our Savior. Amen

PRAYERS OF INTERCESSION
AND COMMEMORATION

God of ____ and ____ [the year that is passing and the year that is opening], Christ of old and of today, Eternal Spirit, hear our prayers for our families as we come to the final days of the old year and prepare to turn the calendar of the new. Whether we are counting the days until we reach retirement age or the next job review and the possibility of promotion, help us to judge our days not in dollar values only but in their usefulness to others, those we work with, those we serve, those we support or help.

Give wisdom to those in positions of responsibility for decisions that make job opportunities for people, that they may provide means for work that are satisfying and constructive for the community at large.

Grant to administrators, teachers, and students a cooperative attitude that can create a setting for learning that will enable each person to achieve his or her fullest potential in organizing, teaching, learning, doing. Grant to coaches and athletes a concern for every individual that healthful activity may encourage full development of skills without unhealthy stress and hateful competitiveness.

Encourage in the mass media a commitment to excellence that seeks to challenge people to serious thinking, sensitive concern for the disadvantaged, careful evaluation in decision making, full responsibility for their own contribution as citizens to the common good.

Renew in all Christian disciples the will to know Christ more clearly, to love him more dearly and follow him more nearly, day by day, year by year, in ____ [upcoming year] and in whatever years are permitted us.

We give you thanks, O God, for all who have fought the good fight and finished the race and kept the faith, and for those dear to us who are at rest with you, especially those who have died in the past year. Grant us grace to follow them as they followed

30

Christ. Bring us, with them, to those things that no eye has seen, nor ear heard, which you have prepared for those who love you. To your name, with the church on earth and the church in heaven, we ascribe all honor and glory, forever and ever. Amen

Second Sunday After Christmas Day

First Lesson - There is reason for joy in the regathering of the people of God after their dispersal. Jeremiah 31:7-14

[OR]

Sirach 24:1-12 The Praise of Wisdom

Psalm 147:12-20

OR

Wisdom 10:15-21

Second Lesson - God's earthly family is adopted through Jesus Christ to enlarge the heavenly family. Ephesians 1:3-14

Gospel - We are a new humanity through Jesus Christ and our rebirth through receiving him. John 1:(1-9), 10-18

CALL TO WORSHIP

Pastor: The grace of our Lord Jesus Christ be with you all.

People: And also with you.

Pastor: Sing out your praises and say,

People: God has saved his people.

INVOCATION

God of our hopes, Christ of our faith, Spirit in our hearts, we come to worship you with joy and gladness. Your goodness knows no limits of generation or gender, of condition or citizenship. You are kind to all and we worship you in all sincerity; through Jesus Christ our Lord. Amen

PRAYER OF CONFESSION

All-glorious God, paternal, fraternal, maternal, we have faith in Jesus Christ, and love toward your people, yet we are not without blemish in your sight, not full of love, wisdom, and other spiritual blessings you still have available for us. Our love is not as inclusive as yours, and there is much we need to learn. Give us clearer vision of all that we are meant to be, so that by becoming fulfilled, we may increase the glory that is properly revealed in Jesus Christ, your beloved. Amen

Declaration of Pardon

Pastor: Friends, hear the good news! The liberator has come to free us from all proud pretenses.

People: The Christ has come in Jesus of Nazareth to show us the undeserved favor of God.

Pastor: Friends, believe the good news!

People: In Jesus Christ, we are forgiven.

[AND]

Exhortation

Accept the limitations of your own knowledge. Have reverence for the wisdom of the Creator. Be thankful for his love in Christ and for a humble place in his house.

PRAYER OF THE DAY

Available God, whatever our age, whether married or single, make us sensitive to what you are doing and about to do, that we may not miss the excitement of being a part of the living history that you are writing, through Jesus Christ. Amen

PRAYER OF THANKSGIVING

We give thanks, God of Job and Jeremiah, David's Lord, Anna's Christ, Luke's savior, that we have found your house in many places. We have found places of prayer with the swallows and the sparrows. We have sung your praise in a quiet circle under the stars. We have enjoyed the choir of many voices and the joyous sounds of musical instruments and found inspiration and refreshment. Along our pilgrim way you provide the cup that sustains both soul and body. We are happy when we trust in you. Amen

PRAYER OF DEDICATION

God of all places, many of us return to this place again and again, expecting spiritual refreshment and growth in grace. Bless all that we do to make this a place of renewal for all who will come to Jesus Christ. Amen

PRAYER OF INTERCESSION
AND COMMEMORATION

God past, God present, God future, continue your governance of the world in which we live. Make your church a potent force for good, overcoming evil with the virtues of the Holy Spirit, conserving the best traditions of the past, adopting the best of new methods of communication and change, anticipating new ways of helping people to help people. Strengthen persons and movements for justice and compassion in our uneven world. Use both governments and volunteer agencies to serve those who need assistance

in feeding the hungry and providing clean water, in pre-
serving life and health, combating disease and healing the
sick, promoting safety and preventing abuse of the weak.

O God, before you the generations rise and pass away.
You are the strength of those who labor; you are the rest of
the blessed dead. We rejoice in the company of your saints.

We remember all who have lived in faith, all who have
peacefully died, and especially those dear to us who rest in
you. Give us in time our portion with those who have trusted in you and have striven to do your holy will. To your
name, with the church on earth and the church in heaven,
we ascribe all honor and glory, now and forever. Amen

Epiphany

First Sunday After the Epiphany (Baptism of Our Lord)

First Lesson - The book of beginnings begins at the beginning. Genesis 1:1-5

Psalm 29

Second Lesson - The more complete experience of the Holy Spirit is granted as the gospel is received in greater fullness. Acts 19:1-7

Gospel - The descent of the dove symbolizes the gift of the Spirit to empower the ministry of Jesus from the beginning. Mark 1:4-11

CALL TO WORSHIP

Leader: The grace of our Lord Jesus Christ be with you all.

People: And also with you.

Leader: Ascribe to the Anointed the glory due to Christ's name.

People: We bow down to the Messiah in the splendor of holiness.

INVOCATION

There are not many of us noble, O God, and our adoration of the Christ Child is more the approach of the shepherds than of the Wise Men. Receive our worship as from the humble, whatever our status in society, as we are unworthy to come before you except through our intermediary whom you sent to us and for us, the Baby of Bethlehem, the Man of Nazareth, Jesus Christ. Amen

PRAYER OF CONFESSION

Creator of what is good, Christ for sinners, Spirit of restoration, we require the baptism of repentance but might not be ready to confess it except that your obedient Son, Jesus, identified himself with us in our sins and showed us your gracious forgiveness signified in the cleansing and refreshing waters of our baptism. Forgive any lack of candidness in our confessions. We need to learn more thoroughgoing honesty before you, ALL-TRUTH, ALL-LEARNING, ALL-LIFE. Amen

Declaration of Pardon

Pastor: Friends, hear the good news! The Holy Spirit is given to us as we put our trust in the name of Jesus Christ our Savior.

People: We have put our trust in the name of Jesus Christ our Savior and the Holy Spirit has been given to us.

Pastor: Friends, believe the good news!

People: In Jesus Christ, we are forgiven.

[AND]

Exhortation

Make your own preparations for the coming of Christ and be ready to give a royal welcome at the return of the scion of heaven and earth.

PRAYER OF THE DAY

Exalted Parent, as you acknowledged your beloved Son, Jesus, so graciously adopt us as your children, being pleased in what your Spirit will yet accomplish in making us more like him to the glory of our family name in Christ. Amen

PRAYER OF THANKSGIVING

Eternal Sovereign, Thunderous Voice, Peace-giving Spirit, we hear the echo of your voice in the majesty of your

Creation and the sob of your grief in what we have thoughtlessly despoiled. Let our thanksgiving be not only the praise we can give to the beauty of what you created, but also the activities we undertake to restore what has been uglified by rapacity and waste. In the restoration of what has been spoiled, may we sense the presence of the Spirit of peace and joy. Amen

PRAYER OF DEDICATION

Powerful Creator, Humble Savior, Renewing Spirit, renew in us the generous nature that is your image in which we were created in the beginning, so that the beauty of the world and the order of the church may be advanced in every generation. Amen

PRAYERS OF INTERCESSION AND COMMEMORATION

God, our helper, uphold us in all times of stress and strain. Sustain those for whom life has become so difficult that they cannot cope any longer. Bless those who have gotten into such a state that the slightest thing irritates and annoys them—those who know it and who cannot help themselves. In turning to you may they relax their tensions and discover the serenity that is proof against the petty pinpricks as well as the shattering blows that life can bring.

Distract those who are worried to the point of obsession with what they cannot change, for which they are not responsible, and which may be beyond all human help. Give them trust for their trembling and hope for their fear.

Bless those whose work has gotten them down so that they are always harassed, disorganized, and never quite able to catch up. Help them to live a day at a time and to take one step at a time; for their confusion give them peace of mind.

Calm those who worry about everything, their health, their work, their children, until the whole of life has become an ordeal. Remind them of your grace, which is sufficient for all human weakness. Bless those who are responsible for most of their own troubles, those who keep putting things off, refusing to make decisions when they are due, and blowing little things out of proportion. Strengthen those too weak to accept criticism, too quick to take offense, or too proud to be open to advice. Grant them insight into themselves so that they may seek from you the help they need.

Bless those in illness, in weariness, and in pain, those who must face a difficult time and after it a long and slow recovery, those who from now on will always have to take things easy, those who are beyond the skill of medicine to help. Give them the patience, the hope, and the courage they need.

Bless those in sorrow, and turn their thoughts to their Lord who brought life and immortality to light.

Bless your church and all who serve it in this land and in lands across the sea, and help your people to find the unity that comes of love of their Lord and love of each other.

Bless our country and the world, and help us to build a land and a world in which all will live in justice and in peace.

Bless our absent friends and dear ones, and when we are anxious about them, help us to remember that, though they are absent from us, they are present with you.

Bless each one of us, and bless all whom we love, and keep us and them in our going out and our coming in, until for us the last day comes and we enter into your nearer presence. Amen

Second Sunday After the Epiphany

First Lesson - The youthful Samuel receives his call to serve as a prophet. 1 Samuel 3:1-20
Psalm 139:1-6, 13-18

Second Lesson - The apostle Paul explains the difference between liberty and license. 1 Corinthians 6:12-20

Gospel - Jesus calls his disciples as he begins his ministry in their company. John 1:43-51

CALL TO WORSHIP

Leader: The grace of our Lord Jesus Christ be with you all.

People: And also with you.

Leader: God's face shines upon us in Christ.

People: We will turn up our faces to him in joy.

INVOCATION

God of Bethel, Christ of Bethlehem, Universal Spirit, your angelic message by Jacob's ladder and the descent of your Son himself to Bethlehem by way of Mary is the beginning of good news that has spread almost everywhere in the world. We worship you because we have responded to that good news with eager faith reborn by the Spirit. Amen

PRAYER OF CONFESSION

Giving God, Uniting God, Indwelling God, we are forgetful of the price you have paid for us in the dying and rising of your Son, Jesus Christ. We sin against our own body and yours when we are not mindful that these bodies, individually and collectively, are shrines for your Holy Spirit. Forgive us if we live too much for food and drink and sex, not disciplined by the Spirit. Save us from all deadly sins by the power that raised Jesus from the dead through your Spirit within us. Amen

Declaration of Pardon

Pastor: Friends, hear the good news! God raised the Lord Jesus.

41

People: **God will also raise us by his saving power.**

Pastor: Friends, believe the good news!

People: **In Jesus Christ, we are forgiven.**

[AND]

Exhortation

When your have heard the call of Jesus to discipleship, follow him, and spend the rest of your life with him.

PRAYER OF THE DAY

Lamb of God, Teacher of disciples, tend us and teach us, that we may live always within sight of you in gentle tractability and learn the simple obedience that will win us a name as reliable followers in your way. Amen

PRAYER OF THANKSGIVING

In broad daylight and in dead of night, in a communal sanctuary and in a quiet mind, you speak our name, God of the covenant, calling us to be your servants. We are honored to serve you and to join with all people who praise you. You have blessed us with all the good things of the earth and granted us the supreme gift of your Spirit to live in us. We would honor you more fully in our bodies, living chastely, devoting our energies to serve you and others, lifting our voices to praise you, shouting in triumph as your justice guides nations. May all people praise you at last, O God, Creator, Judge, Savior/Lord, Holy Spirit. Amen

PRAYER OF DEDICATION

No gift of ours can match the gift of your Spirit, but without our bodies made available and obedient to the Spirit the church cannot be the body of Christ to do your work in the world. Use us and ours as we respond to your call in the gospel of Jesus Christ. Amen

PRAYERS OF INTERCESSION
AND COMMEMORATION

Sovereign God, Living Lord Jesus, Eternal Spirit, we cannot tell what life will bring us but we do believe that you will never leave us, whatever comes. If sorrow comes, comfort us with the hope of glory. If illness comes, help us to bear it gallantly and to reach health again. If disappointment comes, help us always to remember that in spite of everything, the best is always yet to be. If we have to face a hard task or a difficult decision, make us sure that with the challenge there comes the power to do. If we are tempted, help us to turn to the One who was also tempted and who conquered and who can enable us to share his victory. If we are to be misunderstood and unappreciated, help us always to remember that you know us and that it is your verdict that matters. Especially bless those who are in trouble and distress not of their own making: those to whom what has happened is beyond any explanation, that they may accept what they cannot understand; those who have been led astray by someone else, that even yet they may find a way back; those whose background and environment never really gave them a chance. Help them to rise above their circumstances and grant that we who are more fortunate may not rest until we rid this land of conditions in which no one should have to live, in circumstances in which no human being should be entangled.

Bless our world. Help us so solve the clash of color with color, of nation with nation, of creed with creed. And grant that all may turn for leadership to Jesus Christ.

Bless all in authority in our country and in the United Nations. Grant that all may learn to work with diligence and discipline, to seek their pleasure in purity and honor, to remember the things of eternity and not be content with the perishable things of time.

Bless all whom we love and especially those from whom we are separated. Bless each and all of us that we may follow faithfully in the steps of our Lord Jesus Christ until with him we stand before your throne, O God. "Worthy is the Lamb that was slain to receive power and wealth and wisdom and might and honor and glory and blessing!" Amen

Third Sunday After the Epiphany

First Lesson - God urges Jonah a second time to carry a message of repentance through Ninevah after Jonah had evaded the first call. Jonah 3:1-5

Psalm 62:5-12

Second Lesson - Paul is convinced that this world is passing away and all that is temporal fades into insignificance. 1 Corinthians 7:29-31

Gospel - Mark notes the call of the disciples by the preaching of Jesus after the arrest of John the Baptizer. Mark 1:14-20

CALL TO WORSHIP

Leader: The grace of our Lord Jesus Christ be with you all.

People: And also with you.

Leader: Let your heart wait silently before God.

People: Our hope of salvation is in the Eternal One.

INVOCATION

Eternal God, we wait quietly before you, reverently contemplating your majesty and your love for your creation.

Our hope of salvation is the Risen Christ, for the witness of the apostles is the basis for our faith. Through the Spirit of Christ we worship you. Amen

PRAYER OF CONFESSION

God of all times and places, God in Israel and Nazareth, God in our time and place, the meaning of time frequently escapes us. Grief and depression seem like forever. Joy and genuine communion seem so fleeting. Unpleasant duties are postponed; fancied pleasantries are prolonged. Dying takes others away, but we have difficulty facing our own mortality, and evaluating the significance of our own existence. Forgive our disregard for what you intend for us to do and be, for the sake of your temporal and eternal child, Jesus Christ. Amen

Declaration of Pardon

Pastor: Friends, hear the good news! The time has come; the kingdom of God is upon you.

People: We repent and believe Jesus is our Lord.

Pastor: Friends, believe the good news!

People: In Jesus Christ, we are forgiven.

[AND]

Exhortation

Hear the call of Jesus and in following him become a person who, in living with and for others, is fulfilled in time and eternity.

PRAYER OF THE DAY

Master of all occupations, call us from pointless work to purposeful service in your community that we may be fully engaged with the spirit of spreading God's good news, in words and deeds. Amen

PRAYER OF THANKSGIVING

Just God, Loving Lord, Powerful Spirit, we rejoice with all who believe and obey your word on first hearing. We recover our gladness with all who, having heard the word a second time, turn back to do what they were reluctant to do at first hearing. As faithless and frivolous as we may be, you show great patience with us, calling us to discipleship through your Son and our Lord Jesus Christ. How pointed you are about what is not good for us all! How loving is your teaching, living Word! How persuasive is your spirit's dealing with us! We respect your justice. We respond to your love. We are moved by your Spirit. We praise you, O God. Amen

PRAYER OF DEDICATION

Timeless God, since the time we live in will not last long, we would invest both our time and our wealth in the work of your church, which will not pass away. Increase our effectiveness in this company that our cooperative efforts may multiply our individual endeavors, to the glory of your name. Amen

PRAYERS OF INTERCESSION
AND COMMEMORATION

O God, our hearts are restless until they find their rest in you.

O Christ, our hopes are groundless unless they are anchored in you.

Holy Spirit, our prayers are empty except as they are inspired by you.

Comfort, O God, those into whose circle death has come, those in whose eyes there are tears, and on whose heart there is a wound, and who hardly dare to look forward to the road they must tread alone.

Bring relief to those in illness, in weakness, and in pain, those for whom the road back to health is hard and those for whom all hope of recovery is gone.

Challenge those who are allowing some weakness or some habit to become a threat to life itself. Humble those too proud to admit their need of healing that they may yet find recovery and health.

Bring belated wisdom to those who are so busy with things of time that they never think of the things of eternity, those who are so busy working that they have no time for praying.

Give rest to those who are so tired and overworked that they are impatient and irritable and difficult to live with and those for whom life has become a long weariness, one gray day and one grim task after another.

Bless all for whom life is happy, full of interest, rich in friendship, radiant with love. May they give thanksgiving for their blessings.

Maintain your church everywhere in the world, cleansing, reforming, and strengthening it that you may be able to use it for your purposes.

Bless our country and the world community of nations that we may learn to live in peace with justice.

Bless our friends both near and far that we may be true to each other and to you until the days of parting end and we are in eternity with you. To Jesus Christ, the faithful witness, the firstborn of the dead, and the ruler of the kings of the earth, who made us to be a kingdom, with priests serving his God and Father, to him be glory and dominion forever and ever. Amen

Fourth Sunday After the Epiphany

First Lesson - A future prophet is promised, but a warning against false prophets is also issued. Deuteronomy 18:15-20

Psalm 111

Second Lesson - Christian liberty should not be at the expense of the more tender or uncertain Christian conscience. 1 Corinthians 8:1-13

Gospel - Mark portrays demonic competition at the very beginning of the public ministry of healing carried out by Jesus. Mark 1:21-28

CALL TO WORSHIP

Leader: The grace of our Lord Jesus Christ be with you all.

People: And also with you.

Leader: Holy and awesome is the name of God. All who worship have a good understanding.

People: Hallowing God's name is the beginning of wisdom.

INVOCATION

May your praise endure forever, O God, and may our worship be acceptable to you as we hallow your name as did Jesus of Nazareth, your perfect Son. Cleanse us by the inspiration of the Holy Spirit that we may approach you sincerely; through Jesus Christ our Lord. Amen

PRAYER OF CONFESSION

One God, undivided in being, undiverted in purpose, we confess that we are often distracted from waiting on you. Whether married or single, we are easily attracted and engrossed by worldly things. When married or responsible for a family we may have additional cares that divide our minds, giving undue weight to the provision of daily bread and too little attention to what is good, what is seemly, what is true devotion to your work. Forgive faithless anxiety and half-hearted discipleship, unlike your exemplary

Son, Jesus Christ, who was and is dedicated to you in body and in spirit. Amen

Declaration of Pardon

Pastor: Friends, hear the good news! Jesus has power to rid us of unclean spirits.

People: Jesus has power to cast out our sins.

Pastor: Friends, believe the good news!

People: In Jesus Christ, we are forgiven.

[AND]

Exhortation

Be free from anxious care and use your freedom to wait upon the Lord without distraction.

PRAYER OF THE DAY

Jesus of Nazareth, Holy One of God, grant that we may hear the ring of authority in your teaching so that we may be rid of anything that profanes and shackles the human spirit, and be free to serve at your pleasure. Amen

PRAYER OF THANKSGIVING

God of purifying fire, God of true prophets, God of cleansing Spirit, of all the prophets you have sent speaking your word, no one measures up to the true authority of your Son, Jesus Christ. Of all the healers of body, mind, and spirit, none have touched the lives of the sick, the troubled, and the sinful, with as gentle power as Jesus of Nazareth. Of all the scholars and teachers we have known, none have influenced for good as many by their lives and teaching as the Spirit of your Holy Child, Jesus. We are dazzled by visions of your holiness. We are astounded by the deepest revelations of your authority. We are sanctified by the inner baptism of your Spirit. You are worthy of all praise, O God. Amen

PRAYER OF DEDICATION

Lord of the church, we would serve you without distraction, taking the time, and giving the money that is needed, to give genuine expression to the care we have for your business. May it always be our aim to please you, Lord. Amen

PRAYERS OF INTERCESSION AND COMMEMORATION

O God, bless those who have come through, or who are going through, the storms of life. Man of Sorrows and acquainted with grief, Risen Christ, bring the light of resurrection hope to those in the dark night of sorrow; those into whose circle of family or friends death has come, especially if its coming was unexpected.

Healing Christ, bring relief and recovery to those who are sick, especially give patience to those who are chronically ill and a spirit of resignation to those for whom there will be only newness of life after death.

Guide those facing problems that seem insoluble, those facing a parting of the ways that brings to an end familiar patterns of life for the unknown and uncharted ways. Give strength to those are assaulted by temptation, who are fascinated by the wrong thing, who know too well that the spirit is willing but the flesh is weak. May they not surrender, but win out with your help. Restore the joy of living to those who are depressed and for whom life has become a long weariness. Let your praise become the light of their days and nights.

Reunite families and friends who have quarreled and become estranged. May loving forgiveness draw them together again.

Even when life is joyful and full of sunshine, help us to keep uppermost the eternal things that are not changed when night falls or the tides of change sweep away what has been dear to us. Bless your church. Give it wisdom to discern what really matters and not be bogged down in trivia.

Bless our country and give us leaders with ambition to serve the many rather than the few and above all to serve your high purposes.

Bless those we love, especially those from whom we are separated by space or by death that at the last we may be together again where there will be no more parting.

The God of all grace, who has called us to eternal glory in Christ, will restore, support, strengthen, and establish us. To God be the power forever and ever. Amen

Fifth Sunday After the Epiphany

First Lesson - The awesome power of the Creator can be tapped by the person needing strength. Isaiah 40:21-31

Psalm 147:1-11, 20*c*

Second Lesson - The preaching of the gospel for Paul is a kind of compulsion but not without reward. 1 Corinthians 9:16-23

Gospel - The ministry of Jesus is for the healing of body, mind, and spirit. Mark 1:29-39

CALL TO WORSHIP

Leader: The grace of our Lord Jesus Christ be with you all.

People: And also with you.

Leader: O praise the Lord. How good it is to sing psalms to our God!

People: O praise the Lord. How pleasant to praise the Eternal One!

INVOCATION

To sing your praise, O God, is pleasant indeed. To hear other voices joined with ours in common faith and trust in you strengthens our commitment to you through Jesus Christ our Lord. Amen

PRAYER OF CONFESSION

God unlimited, God self-limited, God extending our limits, surely you do not expect us to accept suffering without complaint! We are frustrated with illnesses that rage on, keeping us from doing the things that bring us satisfaction and recognition. Long nights and months of futility seem such a waste to us. Too often we question why it should happen to us, thinking ourselves to be better than others. We forget the exposure of your Son Jesus, to all the circumstances of our mortality. We ignore the spiritual growth that could be ours to prepare us to minister to other sufferers. Forgive our resistance to the healing of spirit and body that your Spirit can enable through our faith in Jesus Christ. Amen

Declaration of Pardon

Pastor: Friends, hear the good news! In the Spirit Jesus still comes, healing those who suffer from various diseases and freeing many who are captives of evil.

People: In the Spirit Jesus still comes bringing healing and freedom.

Pastor: Friends, believe the good news!

People: In Jesus Christ, we are forgiven.

[AND]

Exhortation

Bear your part in spreading the good news, whether in illness or health, weakness or strength, in the service of God.

PRAYER OF THE DAY

Synagogue-preacher, sick-bed-visitor, exorcist-of-evil, so teach us, so heal us, so clear us of evil, that we may be ready learners and teachers, visitors of the sick and the shut-in, of other sinners, gathering around you in one needy company. Amen

PRAYER OF THANKSGIVING

Creator of stars, nurse to the wounded, healer of broken spirits: that you have power to rule the cosmos, fills us with awe. That you stoop to touch and heal us, fills us with amazement. You give new heart to the humble. We thank you for all that sustains life, whether human, vegetable, or animal. Receive the thanksgiving of all creation, the psalms of your people, the music of the birds, the sounds of all living things. Hear us wherever we gather to praise your name. Amen

PRAYER OF DEDICATION

God of the gospel, we share the responsibility of spreading the good news, with pastors and elders, evangelists and teachers, healers and nurses, identifying with all sorts and conditions of people in order to communicate the word of your grace in Jesus Christ. Amen

PRAYERS OF INTERCESSION
AND COMMEMORATION

Fatherly God, Brotherly Christ, Motherly Spirit, embrace and help any who are troubled today. Lighten the darkness of those in grief. Send them comforters in their loneliness and reminders that the day of parting is past and the day of meeting again will come.

Give courage to try again to those who have lost jobs or squandered their money. Bless those to whom any disappointment has come, those who have experienced the failure of friendship or of love, and keep them from all bitterness.

Show your kindness to those who face shame and disgrace, who have made mistakes for which they have had to pay bitterly, and help them to use the future to atone for the past.

Guide those for whom this is a crucial time: those who are beginning new studies or new jobs, those who for the first time have to leave home to work in another place, those who are beginning the retirement phase of their lives and leaving behind familiar patterns of work, those who have become engaged or who are about to be married, those who cannot determine whether they should marry, those who are awaiting the birth of their first child and the first responsibilities of parenting.

Bless our country and help us as a nation to follow justice and peace.

Bless your church in all its branches around the world. Unite us all in the bonds of peace.

Bless all whom we love, especially those from whom we are separated, and keep us all in your care and in the community of the faithful in Jesus Christ, who is the Way, the Truth, and the Life. Amen

Sixth Sunday After the Epiphany

First Lesson - Simple obedience to the will of God is sometimes the way to new health and strength. 2 Kings 5:1-14

Psalm 30

Second Lesson - There is an eternal prize for the moral discipline of our bodies as well as our minds. 1 Corinthians 9:24-27

Gospel - Jesus is a healer with great compassion for the sick and ready to touch the "untouchable." Mark 1:40-45

CALL TO WORSHIP

Leader: The grace of our Lord Jesus Christ be with you all.

People: And also with you.

Leader: Rejoice and be glad, good people.

People: We will rejoice and sing aloud before our Sovereign.

INVOCATION

If we have come to you, O God, in sorrow, comfort us; if in depression, lift us up; if in anger, release us from our animosity; that we may truly worship you with joy and gratitude for your grace in Christ Jesus our Lord. Amen

PRAYER OF CONFESSION

God most high, God most humble, God most honest, forgive the pride that prevents us from repenting and being healed of our sins, the pride of place that will not let us appreciate the virtues of other places, the pride of race that scorns the accomplishments of other nationalities, the personal pride that will not respect the rights and privileges of others. We need the honesty to be humble with all and subservient to none but you, after the example Jesus Christ. Amen

Declaration of Pardon

Pastor: Friends, hear the good news! As you have shown yourself willing to come to Christ,

People: we will be forgiven and cleansed of all our sins.

Pastor: Friends, believe the good news!

People: In Jesus Christ, we are forgiven.

[AND]

Exhortation

Strive for spiritual excellence as an athlete trains and competes for less enduring laurels.

PRAYER OF THE DAY

Healing and humble Christ, help us to serve the needs of others without concern for the attention and praise of the many, content to know that we have responded to the cry for help. Amen

PRAYER OF THANKSGIVING

Gracious God, guiltless Christ, gladdening Spirit, our joy is in knowing that you are forgiving and do not hold our sins against us forever. When we give up the attempted concealment of our guilt, you enfold us in your saving and loving arms, putting our sin and guilt behind us. We find refuge with you in times of distress that come as great floods threatening to sweep us away. We rejoice in your unfailing love. Amen

PRAYER OF DEDICATION

Generous God, though there is no way we can repay you for your kindness and mercy in Jesus Christ, receive our offerings as a token of gratitude and enable us to share the good news with others through this community. Amen

PRAYERS OF INTERCESSION AND COMMEMORATION

Unforgetting God, Compassionate Christ, Consoling Spirit, we intercede for those we may otherwise forget or ignore knowing that you remember and bless and comfort. Especially today we pray for those in illness, weakness, or pain, those recovering from accident, those losing their hearing or their sight, sick children who do not know what is happening to them, young people facing lifetime limitations, middle-aged people whose failing health jeopardizes their own livelihood and their family, aged ones on whom the last shadows are darkening, those for whom there is nothing but to watch and wait and pray.

Comfort those in sorrow. Dry their tears and lift their eyes to eternity and the reunion awaiting us. Strengthen those who are aware of their weakness in resisting temptation and give them courage instead of fear.

Bless those who set their hearts on something they can never have and who live in disappointment and defeat.

Bless those who worry about their loved ones, about their health, about shrinking income and increasing expense, and about the day that may never come.

Teach us to trust in your care and to live a day at a time. Bless your church here and everywhere. What is dark in it illumine; what is wanting supply; what is in error correct; what is without energy empower. Bless our country and community with leaders who follow you. Bless our loved ones and absent friends. Keep us in the communion of your saints on earth and in heaven through Jesus Christ our Lord. Amen

Seventh Sunday After the Epiphany

First Lesson - Spiritual transformation, not merely new rituals, are what the Eternal One desires from God's people. Isaiah 43:18-25

Psalm 41

Second Lesson - The greatest affirmative action in history is the sending of Jesus as the confirmation of God's gracious promises. 2 Corinthians 1:18-22

Gospel - Only God has the final authority to forgive our sins and that authority was shared with the Son of Man, Jesus of Nazareth. Mark 2:1-12

CALL TO WORSHIP

Leader: The grace of our Lord Jesus Christ be with you all.

People: And also with you.

Leader: In Christ Jesus every one of God's promises is a "Yes."

People: For this reason through him we say the "Amen," to the glory of God.

INVOCATION

Covenant God, you promise life eternal to us through your perfect Son, Jesus Christ. We give glory to you, Father, Son, and Holy Spirit. We confess that we do not always say "yes" to you but today in our worship we say, "Amen." Amen

PRAYER OF CONFESSION

Patient Parent, holy and forgiving, we would rather speak to those who speak to us, to love those who love us in return. We enjoy the common enthusiasms of our own country and its people. We would rather hate our enemies than pray for them and for those who harass us. The passive resistance that Jesus teaches seems unworkable to us and unfair, giving the advantage to our adversaries, at the expense of our personal rights. Forgive us for following our own devices and not obeying the instruction of Jesus Christ. Amen

Declaration of Pardon

Pastor: Friends, hear the good news! To us as to others, Jesus says, "Your sins are forgiven."

People: To us as to others, Jesus says, "Your sins are forgiven."

Pastor: Friends, believe the good news!

People: In Jesus Christ, we are forgiven.

[AND]

Exhortation

Do not bear hatred for your brothers and sisters in your heart. Do not take revenge or cherish grudges. The Lord says to love your neighbor as yourself.

PRAYER OF THE DAY

Your goodness, O God, knows no bounds. Increase our goodness beyond its present limits to higher stages of maturity, that our love and forgiveness may become more nearly like that of your Son, our Savior, Jesus Christ. Amen

PRAYER OF THANKSGIVING

Gracious God, your benevolence is not limited to the deserving or those who would receive the many benefits that we take for granted. You make your sun to rise on good and bad alike and send the rain on the honest and the dishonest. We are grateful for all your gifts and for the friendships that have come to us without our seeking them, for those who have been kind and helpful to us without any initiative on our part. Help us to show our thankfulness by taking the initiative in reaching out to others who need friends, by going the extra mile to be helpful, especially for those who may not be able to ask for help. We appreciate being part of your family gathered in the Spirit. We are humbled by the thought that as we belong to Christ, we belong to you, God of all. Amen

PRAYER OF DEDICATION

You honor us, Divine Spirit, by making your home within us. Make us more fitting temples for your habitation, urging us toward the maturity and open-heartedness that is the genius of our Divine Parent. Bless our church as a means to that end, through Jesus Christ our Lord. Amen

PRAYERS OF INTERCESSION AND COMMEMORATION

God our Creator, Christ sometime Carpenter, Spirit at work in the church, hear our prayers for all who work.

Bless those who serve the public in shops and in offices, those in transport by road, by sea, by air, those who work in restaurants and hotels, and grant that they may combine efficiency with courtesy and consideration.

Bless those who work in industry, in factories and shipyards, in mines and quarries, in all the many crafts and trades that we depend on, and grant they may have honest satisfaction in their work and fair remuneration for their labor.

Bless those who teach the young and the old, in schools and colleges and universities, in clubs and fellowships, in workshops and seminars, and grant that they may help to teach us how to live as well as how to make a living.

Bless those who heal our bodies and ease our pains—doctors and physicians, surgeons, dentists, specialists, nurses, therapists with many skills—that they may serve in the spirit of the great healer, Jesus Christ.

Bless also those who heal our minds and nerves—psychiatrists and psychotherapists, counselors and leaders of self-help groups—that they may listen carefully and respond wisely and sympathetically and treat skillfully.

Bless those who make and administer our laws—lawyers, legislators, police officers, magistrates, judges, justices, prison-officers, and governors—that they may seek to rehabilitate as well as to punish and that they be kept safe in hazardous duty.

Bless all who perform public services, whether paid or volunteer, who fight fires, who operate ambulance services, who maintain our streets, who operate our sanitary systems, and protect our community health, that they may be appreciated for their contribution to our common good.

Bless those who write and publish books, newspapers, and magazines, and those who write for and speak in the various mass media, that they may be devoted to truth and seek to be an influence for the good of all.

Bless dramatists and moviemakers, cartoonists and artists, dancers and singers, that the lively arts may not only bring us pleasure but also grace and beauty.

Bless those who serve the church in the ministry of Word and Sacrament, in church education, in administration, in music and all the activities that make up our total life together, that your Lordship may always be recognized in all we do and how we do it.

Bless homemakers whose work is never done, all who have the responsibility for care of children and family, and community services that support the aged in their own or communal homes.

Bless us each one. When we speak, may we do so as those speaking your very words, as we serve, may we do so with the strength that you supply, so that you, O God, may be glorified in all things through Jesus Christ, to whom with you and the Holy Spirit belongs the glory and the power forever and ever. Amen

Transfiguration

First Lesson - Elijah is translated from earthly to heavenly service and Elisha succeeds him. 2 Kings 2:1-12

Psalm 50:1-6

Second Lesson - The light of God is most clearly focused in the face of Jesus Christ, writes Paul. 2 Corinthians 4:3-6

Gospel - Jesus is transfigured in the eyes of the inner circle of the twelve. Mark 9:2-9

CALL TO WORSHIP

Leader: The grace of our Lord Jesus Christ be with you all.

People: And also with you.

Leader: Gather to Christ, Christians, for he has given himself to make a new covenant with all of us.

People: His self-sacrifice has established the new testament, which includes all believers.

INVOCATION

God of promise, Christ the promised One, Holy Spirit from God to the church of the promise, we come to worship you as we are drawn by the Spirit into the community of the new covenant in Jesus Christ. Bless your people wherever they are gathered in the name of Jesus Christ. Amen

PRAYER OF CONFESSION

God of the gospel, Christ of God, Spirit of God, forgive us if we become enamored of others, great as they are, and do not center our lives and our loyalties on the One who is your beloved Son. Excuse our enthusiasms for lesser luminaries, the gods of our passing age, whose fascination and fame may distract us from following Jesus Christ with undivided devotion. Amen

Declaration of Pardon

Pastor: Friends, hear the good news! The gospel of the glory of Christ, who is the very image of God, has dawned upon us

People: **so that we can avoid the way to perdition.**

Pastor: Friends, believe the good news!

People: **In Jesus Christ, we are forgiven.**

[AND]

Exhortation

Proclaim not yourselves nor any institution instead of Jesus Christ as Lord and ourselves his servants.

PRAYER OF THE DAY

Transfiguring Spirit, clear our sight of all unbelief so that in seeing Christ in all his divine perfection we may worship him exclusively and look for no other leader into the realm of God. Amen

PRAYER OF THANKSGIVING

Speaking God, shining God, Judging God, we celebrate the beauty and order of the world, which you have summoned into being. We respect the justice that you proclaim in the orderliness of the heavens and that you seek to restore among us in the revelation of your glory in the face of Jesus Christ. We give thanks for all who have passed along the heritage of faith and the call to serve you. We will hallow your name forever and for no other. Amen

PRAYER OF DEDICATION

Infinite God, your presence is confined by no shelter, nor can all nature radiate your glory. Reveal your gracious glory again in the face of Jesus Christ and in the works of his body the church. Amen

PRAYERS OF INTERCESSION
AND COMMEMORATION

God of all worlds, Christ the human image of God, Divine Spirit shared not only with prophets, but all believers in Jesus Christ, like the young prophet Elisha, we desire a fuller empowerment of the Spirit not only in the elders, but in all your people. As we are drawn apart from the busy world, give us a more glorious vision of your holy love that we may go out into the world again with joyful sharing of the grace so freely given. Having seen the personal perfection of beauty, in Jesus Christ grant us Divine Spirit to let your radiance shine forth.

May our neighbors and colleagues at work, our business associates and customers, our kinfolk and friends know from our attitudes toward them and life in general that we have been with you and you have spoken to us out of the silence. May we bring others to gather around the Lord's Table to receive the sacrament of the new covenant with all earth's people made by the sacrifice of Jesus on the cross.

In the world of politics, so often clouded with greed for power and wealth, bring a vision of the Suffering Servant whose love for people in poverty and disease brought compassion and institutions for education and healing and mutual help. Prevent us from confusing any partisan political agenda with the guidelines that Jesus taught and the example of life as he lived it among us.

As Jesus was a healer and miracle worker, so continue, through the church and all your apostles, ministries that transfigure outcasts with the dignity of the children of God, that transform the addicted to the freedom of minds and bodies made whole, and that convert the doubtful and unbelieving to joyful faith.

As we remember with thanksgiving the prophets and apostles and leaders of the church in every age, hear our commitment to continue their witness in the world to the light that has shone for us in the face of Jesus Christ. Keep us truly alive in the faith that the chain that binds us together cannot be broken by death, and that at the last your people from all times and places will bring glory to your name. Amen

Lent

First Sunday in Lent

First Lesson - God established with Noah the covenant of the rainbow. Genesis 9:8-17

Psalm 25:1-10

Second Lesson - Peter says that the water of the flood and the water of baptism both take away sin. 1 Peter 3:18-22

Gospel - After his baptism by John the Baptizer Jesus begins forty days of temptation in the wilderness. Mark 1:9-15

CALL TO WORSHIP

Leader: The grace of our Lord Jesus Christ be with you all.

People: And also with you.

Leader: Look for signs of the covenant that God makes with us and our children to endless generations.

People: No one who hopes in God will be put to shame.

INVOCATION

Creator of sunshine and rain, Christ of pleasure and pain, Spirit of virtuous gain, we worship you as those who look for rainbows as evidence of your covenant of mercy not to destroy but to renew and reform us and our creation spoiled by greed and careless use. Receive us with the intercession of Jesus Christ, for his sake. Amen

PRAYER OF CONFESSION

Savior-God, at whose right hand sits the Risen Christ, having received the submission of angels; without our baptism we could not come before you in good conscience. Without the death of Christ for our sins, we would be condemned.

We are among the unjust for whom the just Christ willingly suffered. Our only hope of salvation is in the resurrection of Jesus Christ, who was put to death in the body and brought to life in the Spirit. Were it not for that good news, we too would be imprisoned by our sin and guilt. Grant us continuing repentance and faith in the gospel; under the rainbow of your covenant and our baptism in the name of the Father, and of the Son, and of the Holy Spirit. Amen

Declaration of Pardon

Pastor: Friends, hear the good news! Christ died for our sins once and for all.

People: He, the just, suffered for the unjust to bring us to God.

Pastor: Friends, believe the good news!

People: In Jesus Christ, we are forgiven.

[AND]

Exhortation

Through these forty days and all the days of your life, resist the temptations of God's adversaries, in the strength that God is willing to give you.

PRAYER OF THE DAY

God of imprisoned prophets, so rule in our hearts that we may turn back from every evil way and, believing the gospel, be sent by the Spirit to people and places where the good news has yet to come; in the name of Jesus Christ. Amen

PRAYER OF THANKSGIVING

Creator of all life, Person from whom comes all persons, Maker of covenants, we see in the rainbow your promise never to destroy all life by flood. We find in the church an ark to save us from spiritual death. We give thanks to you for the continuing sign of baptism to remind us of the death and resurrection of Jesus Christ, the just for the unjust to bring us to you. We rejoice that he is at your right hand, being raised to high honor, after receiving the submission of angelic authorities and powers. May all living things praise you. May all persons worship and obey you. May all parties who covenant with you keep their faith, or renew their promises, through Jesus Christ our Lord. Amen

PRAYER OF DEDICATION

Holy God, we are unworthy to stand before you except by the grace of our baptism. Sanctify our gifts by the Spirit that they may be worthy of your use in the proclamation of the good news of Jesus Christ. Amen

PRAYERS OF INTERCESSION
AND COMMEMORATION

God of Creation, at our end of the rainbow, help us to wisely use the world in which we live. Bless all who are at work protecting the wetlands and forests to preserve the birds, the domestic animals, and every animal of the earth. Help our government and businesses to maintain a proper balance for the need of development and employment with the needs of all humanity for clear water and clean air.

Bless our schools that our students may be taught the intricacies of nature that they may learn respect for your creation and for their own bodies. Teach all of us to love our neighbors as we love ourselves and to share what we have with those who have little.

Preserve your church and enliven us with the Spirit that we may provide an ark of salvation amid the rising floods of hopelessness. May our deeds as well as our words bring light and hope to the dark corners of our common life.

Hear our prayers for our families, our neighbors, our friends who are sick at this time. Grant them health and strength according to their day, that they may rejoice in your healing balm. Grant them patience of spirit during the time of their healing that they may be stronger spiritually as well.

Bless all who are in authority over us that they may use their powers with the acknowledgment that they are accountable to you if not to us for what they do or fail to do.

God our Savior, through the resurrection of Jesus Christ, you have taken our holy Brother, Jesus, to your right hand, with angels and authorities, and powers made subject to him. We remember with thanksgiving those known and dear to us who have received a like resurrection to your heavenly circle. By the Spirit, keep us in touch with the family of God on earth and in heaven that together we may serve you in the beauty of holiness, always hallowing your name. Amen

Second Sunday in Lent

First Lesson - Abram's name is changed to Abraham as God makes a covenant with him to provide a successor/son through Sarah his wife. Genesis 17:1-7, 15-16

Psalm 22:23-31

Second Lesson - Paul uses the example of Abraham and Sarah as a model of trust in God's promises of salvation. Romans 4:13-25

Gospel - Jesus rebukes the idea that his mission can be accomplished without suffering and says that all disciples have a cross to bear. Mark 8:31-38

CALL TO WORSHIP

Leader: The grace of our Lord Jesus Christ be with you all.

People: **And also with you.**

Leader: Let all who see God be joyful in heart and exult in the hallowed name.

People: **We will live in the divine presence always as a source of our strength.**

INVOCATION

Wise, just, and merciful God, we seek you with joyful hearts because you have been revealed to us through Jesus Christ. We hallow your name in the prayer he taught us and by our worship enabled by your Holy Spirit. Hear our prayers and our hymns of praise in Jesus' name. Amen

PRAYER OF CONFESSION

Divine Thinker, Messianic Sufferer, Loving Spirit, we confess that we long for glory but avoid suffering. To be recognized and praised pleases us, but we turn back from the cross of unpleasant truth-telling and the defense of unpopular causes. Forgive our unwillingness to follow Christ in carrying our own crosses and living the truth as your Spirit would do if we willingly submitted to such guidance. Pardon pride and the sinful advice that we give others who are prepared to be humble like Jesus, in whose name we pray. Amen

Declaration of Pardon

Pastor: Friends, hear the good news! Like Abraham's faith in God, our faith can be counted for the good,

People: **because Jesus was given up to death for our misdeeds and raised from the dead to justify us in the sight of God.**

Pastor: Friends, believe the good news!
People: In Jesus Christ, we are forgiven.

[AND]

Exhortation

Hear the call of Jesus to be a disciple. Bear your cross bravely and risk your life that in the end you may be saved.

PRAYER OF THE DAY

Christ of Cross and Crown, strengthen us in unselfishness and in faith that in this wicked and godless age, we may be faithful disciples in both word and deed and thus honor your name and the name given us in our baptism. Amen

PRAYER OF THANKSGIVING

God of patriarch and matriarch, of disciple and unbeliever, we are thankful for the call of Jesus to believe in him and to share in the acceptance you grant to all who believe in him. We would thank you by our actions as well as our adoration, by our service as well as our prayers, our offerings as well as our promises. What noble but human ancestors in the faith you have given us to set an example of what can be done by you when your people are willing. We praise your grace and give glory to your name. Amen

PRAYER OF DEDICATION

Matchless Giver, receive our offerings of ourselves and our possession, insignificant beside the gift of Christ, but precious to you as signs of our obedient cross-bearing hallowed by the Spirit. Amen

PRAYERS OF INTERCESSION AND COMMEMORATION

Ancient of Days, Man of the Hour, Spirit Eternal, what you created you sustain in orderly fashion, and what you loved to life you have joined in the entry into our history in Christ. Grant that all who trace to Abraham and Sarah their faith in one God, the love for one another that will seek reconciliation among synagogue and church and mosque, that the world that dies all deity will consider more thoughtfully the faith that we have in common.

Especially bless the church to which we belong that we may make strong the ties that bind us to others of like precious faith and live up to the high calling that is ours in Christ Jesus. May we convey this faith by daily prayer in our homes as well as Sunday prayers in your house.

Grant to our nation more tolerance of differences racial, ethnic, social, economic, and religious, that we may attain a greater harmony in our common life and less violence on our streets. To those who monitor our streets and highways and waterways, grant wisdom and caution as they meet threats to our common safety.

Bless with your compassionate Spirit the medical community with the vocation to heal the sick. Grant that the businesses providing the systems for our healthcare may know the concern for persons as well as profits in order to to bring us what is needed with fairness to all, both rich and poor.

God of eternity, Christ for all times, Timeless Spirit, we rejoice in the communion of saints who from the time of Abraham and Sarah have worshiped you and brought up their children to trust you as they followed your leading in life. We give thanks especially for those we have known in our own lifetime who have taught us by word and example to be ardent disciples of Jesus Christ. We honor those who are still with us and commemorate the lives of those now in the heavenly realm. Bring us at last into that perfect society unblemished by conflict or misunderstanding and totally worshipful in the kingdom of love, through Jesus Christ our Lord, to whom with you Eternal One be all glory and praise. Amen

Third Sunday in Lent

First Lesson - Moses discloses the covenant God makes with the former slaves brought out of Egypt. Exodus 20:1-17

Psalm 19:1-14

Second Lesson - Paul affirms to the Corinthians the strength and wisdom of God over against the weakness and foolishness of humanity. 1 Corinthians 1:18-25

Gospel - Jesus cleanses the Temple by chasing out the commercial entrepreneurs. John 2:13-22

CALL TO WORSHIP

Leader: The grace of our Lord Jesus Christ be with you all.

People: And also with you.

Leader: God calls us to faith in the Christ nailed to the cross, as wisdom wiser than ours and power stronger than ours.

People: We hear God's call to the teaching and example of Jesus.

INVOCATION

God of majesty, Christ of humility, Spirit of unanimity, no one can boast in the your presence. We may not be wise by human standards, powerful in society, or noble in birthright, but we come to you in Christ, who is our wisdom, our virtue, our Redeemer, who alone is our boast. Amen.

PRAYER OF CONFESSION

God of the law, Christ of the cross, Spirit of purity, we confess that we have broken your commandments, commercialized your church, compromised the simplicity of the faith. We are too ready to choose our favorite commandments and to ignore the others to minimize our guilt. We excuse our breaking of some of them by pointing out that we are keeping the others. Forgive any self-righteousness that ignores the need for the sacrifice of Christ for our sins and the cleansing of the Spirit for our holiness. Amen.

Declaration of Pardon

Pastor: Friends, hear the good news! God is not only lawgiver but redeemer

People: and will cleanse us from the secret sins that have escaped our own attention.

Pastor: Friends, believe the good news!

People: In Jesus Christ, we are forgiven.

[AND]

Exhortation

Be enlightened by all that God commands. Your spirit will be revived by God's law and you will find reward in the keeping of the commandments.

PRAYER OF THE DAY

Let our zeal for your house, Lord Jesus, be exceeded only by our desire to be pure in heart and thus enabled to see you in your ultimate glory. Amen

PRAYER OF THANKSGIVING

God of wisdom, we praise your name. Christ of the cross, we give thanks for your loving and forgiving death for our sins. Purifying Spirit, we celebrate the liberation from our guilt as you renew and revive our spirits. We are humbled by the dignity to which you call us despite our faults and failing. Thanks be to you, O God. Amen

PRAYER OF DEDICATION

Your house, O God, is meant to be a house of prayer. May nothing we do here be inappropriate to that purpose, but be supportive of your design in Jesus Christ. Amen

PRAYERS OF INTERCESSION AND COMMEMORATION

God above but not beyond us; Jesus of history, Christ of glory; Spirit of God's presence: may our Lenten penitence be more than a seasonal commitment to humility before you. In renewing our covenant relationship with you, may the church be as aware of the needs of today as your people were in the forty years of their wandering and the giving of the Old Covenant at Sinai.

Bless all evangelists and teachers who proclaim that covenant and the new covenant that Jesus sealed with the blood of his cross. With the good news of your grace in Jesus Christ, order the lives of your people in the spirit of the Risen Christ who taught the perfect law of love.

Divine Physician, you heal our bodies, minds, and spirits, curing our ills, calming our minds, renewing our spirits. Grant your healing to all who look to you for complete wholeness and holiness.

In our democratic society, grant each of us as citizens a proper sense of our obligations to participate in the electoral process, joining with neighbors in the search for good candidates for public office. Help us to be good citizens and cooperative volunteers in groups and agencies that serve the needs of others.

As you have provided for a day of rest in each week of work, you have also created a rest that remains for your children. We rejoice in the completion of the work of those you have called to their final Sabbath and seek to serve you faithfully throughout our own lifetimes. Then give us joy together again in your heavenly garden where blooms the tree with leaves for the healing of the nations. We will give glory to you, heartily, Fatherly, Brotherly, Motherly God, One God for ever. Amen.

Fourth Sunday in Lent

First Lesson - This is a story that Jesus will retell in his talk with Nicodemus. Numbers 21:4-9

Psalm 107:1-3, 17-22

Second Lesson - Paul describes the spiritual resurrection of believers by the grace of God's salvation. Ephesians 2:1-10

Gospel - John completes the discourse of Jesus with Nicodemus on the nature of salvation, switching from the rebirth analogy to a judicial parallel. John 3:14-21

CALL TO WORSHIP

Leader: The grace of our Lord Jesus Christ be with you all.

People: And also with you.

Leader: Do not avoid the light of God but expose yourself to it.

People: We come to the light so that it will be clear that

God is involved in all the good things that we do.

INVOCATION

Holy God, you did not send your Son into the world to condemn the world, but in order that the world might be saved through him. We believe in him and are not condemned, so we come with our thanksgivings and our petitions in the name of the only perfect Son of God, Jesus Christ. Amen

PRAYER OF CONFESSION

Ruler of our enemies and our allies, adversary of evil everywhere, Savior of all who put their trust in you, we confess that we do not always turn your light on ourselves as carefully as on the behavior of others. We are too prone to spotlight the failures and injustices of societies other than our own. In our private lives we have been subject to the whims of our sensual natures convinced that the natural is always good, ignoring your prohibitions against what is hurtful to both others and ourselves. Forgive our incomplete obedience to your prompting and save us from our sins by your grace in Jesus Christ. Amen

Declaration of Pardon

Pastor: Friends, hear the good news! God is rich in mercy, for the great love he bore us

People: brought us to life with Christ even when we were dead in ours sins; it is by his grace that we are saved.

Pastor: Friends, believe the good news!

People: In Jesus Christ, we are forgiven.

[AND]

80

Exhortation

Devote yourselves to the good deeds for which God has designed you.

PRAYER OF THE DAY

Divine descendant from heaven, human ascendant from earth, let the light of love from your cross continue to shine in our world so that all who look to you in faith may live, no longer under judgment, but in grateful allegiance to you. Amen

PRAYER OF THANKSGIVING

Gracious Sovereign, we praise the mercy that you have shown to your rebel subjects who have returned to live under your loving rule. Divine treasurer, we are thankful for all the resources of your grace that enrich our lives. Divine designer, we celebrate the handiworks you have created, retooling us to accomplish the purpose of your realm. You have brought us out of death into life, out of subservience to evil, into the freedom of all that is godly and good. How great is your kindness to us in Jesus Christ. Amen

PRAYER OF DEDICATION

No sanctuary is worthy of you, O God, but we bring our offerings not only to furnish this house of prayer, but to manifest to the world the gift of salvation that you freely offer in Jesus Christ. Amen

PRAYERS OF INTERCESSION AND COMMEMORATION

Loving God, we pray for the world that you created and loved, seeing it in the beginning to be good. Continue your forbearance with all humanity and by the grace of our Lord

Jesus Christ, bring back to yourself and your ways those you are redeeming from trouble and are gathering in from the lands, from the east and from the west, from the north and from the south. Some were sick through their sinful ways, and because of their iniquities endured affliction. Grant healing and restoration.

In this Lenten season, purify the church, member by member, that we may be free of the spirit that is still at work among those who are disobedient. Raise us up again to be seated with him in the heavenly places in Christ Jesus. From such mountaintop transfiguration lead us out into the community to do the good works, which God prepared beforehand to be our way of life.

Bless every ministry that feeds the hungry and provides clothing and shelter for the homeless and refugee. Send healers to the sick in lands not blessed with as many doctors and nurses as we have here. Guide and bless international agencies concerned with the health of babies and people in underdeveloped nations on our globe.

Hear our prayer for our own sick. Grant success to special ministries with the blind, the hearing impaired, the slow learner, the emotionally disturbed. Help us to provide adequate funding, public or private, for these and other agencies.

Make our government amenable to the needs of rich and poor, weak and strong, male and female, employer and employee, that we may work together in harmony and good faith.

Grant grace, mercy, and peace to all who maintain hospices for the dying. May we live serenely and come to the end of life in serenity.

We rejoice in the hope of everlasting life with you, loving God, and with the whole community you gather around you. We celebrate the assembly of the firstborn who are enrolled in heaven, and pray to be brought at last to the community of the righteous made perfect by the grace of our Lord Jesus Christ. Amen

Fifth Sunday in Lent

First Lesson - The prophet Jeremiah forecasts a new covenant of the heart to replace the broken one. Jeremiah 31:31-34

Psalm 51:1-12

Second Lesson - Jesus is praised as a sincere and suffering high priest appointed by God to serve all who obey him. Hebrews 5:5-10

Gospel - John reports the interest of some Greeks as the occasion for the explanation by Jesus of what suffering love will accomplish in the divine purpose. John 12:20-33

CALL TO WORSHIP

Leader: The grace of our Lord Jesus Christ be with you all.

People: And also with you.

Leader: Come to see Jesus, even though his glory is a cross.

People: We will follow him and carry a cross of our own.

INVOCATION

Suffering God, crucified Christ, healing Spirit, we worship you because we know you to be compassionate, forgiving, and regenerating. We rejoice in the new covenant you have made with us all, in Jesus Christ your Son, our Redeemer. Amen

PRAYER OF CONFESSION

Renewer of covenants, divine-human Pledge of the new covenant, Spirit of the covenant, forgive our wrongdoing and remember our sins against us no more. Though you are known by the high and the lowly, we have not reached the time when it will not be necessary to teach one another to know you. Or is it that knowing you, we decline to obey you? As you were patient with Israel and Judah when they broke your covenant, we implore your patience with us, who are the children of the new covenant, made with the world in the cross of Jesus Christ, your Son. Much of what we know has not yet been incorporated in our lives and we need a willing Spirit, new and steadfast like your obedient child, Jesus. Amen

Declaration of Pardon

Pastor: Friends, hear the good news! God has named as our high priest, the Son who learned obedience and was made perfect in suffering.

People: Jesus Christ has become the source of eternal salvation to all who obey him.

Pastor: Friends, believe the good news!

People: In Jesus Christ, we are forgiven.

[AND]

Exhortation

Follow the Son of Man, that where Christ is, you may serve, and in serving be honored by our Divine Parent.

PRAYER OF THE DAY

Christ of the cross, drive out the prince of this world from strongholds in and around us, that being freed from the hold of evil we may be drawn to you and glorify your name and the name of the One who sent you. Amen

PRAYER OF THANKSGIVING

God of justice, delivering champion, purifying Spirit, you give us joy in remembering our deliverance from the power of the evil one through the victory of Christ and the Cross. You have not driven us from you, but created pure hearts within us that we might remain near you. We will sing the praise of your justice and commit ourselves to teach the way that leads to you, to other transgressors, who may also turn to you again and know the joy of your salvation. Receive our praise, God of old and new covenants, through Christ our high priest and by the Holy Spirit. Amen

PRAYER OF DEDICATION

We would be your people, O God, as you have offered to be our God. Through your church, lift up your Son, Jesus, as a continuing high priest interceding for all sinners, to the glory of your name. Amen

PRAYERS OF INTERCESSION AND COMMEMORATION

Creator and Judge of the world, Advocate and Savior of the world, Conscience and Remaker of the world, hear our prayers for the world that stands under judgment for the fracture of covenants of law and grace that you have made with human society. Drive out the evil one who draws together forces of hatred and genocide and cleanse us and our society from the prejudices that fail to measure others as we measure ourselves. Confront with your justice the anarchists who resist justice with laws of their own making. Replace the hard heart and the narrow construction of what is righteous, with the reverent knowledge of you and your justice with mercy that will bring heaven to earth and earth to heaven.

Make your church an example of love at work with reverence alike for you and the humanity that you have created male/female in your image. May your church be as young as the newest baptized member and as old as the most aged worshiper. May our life together be open to all who need our company in your presence, whatever their age or personality.

May our government be open to the best from every culture and religious tradition, providing the means for educating our young of both limited and unlimited potential. Keep us all young in learning so that we do not grow resistant to change that can benefit the greatest number by the reordering of our society.

Grant to thinkers and planners the vision to organize our work and play for the profit and benefit of all, with none overworked and others left idle in the marketplace without a job and without the dignity of meaningful participation in our common life.

Though we may learn from our suffering as Jesus did, may we know the healing arts that he practiced in his life among us. Grant to all who need it healing of body, mind, and spirit through the ministries of the church, the medical professions, and healthcare institutions.

Bless all who are healers with your loving wisdom and grant to all patients trust in your goodness and patience with those who care for them.

God of yesterday, today, and forever, you have given us hope for what we do not yet see, so grant us patience to wait for it. We rejoice with those who have already realized your final grace and salvation. May we live daily in expectation of your faithful fulfillment of the promises in our baptism and the sacrament of the bread and the cup. We will hallow your name, today and in eternity. Amen

Sixth Sunday in Lent

First Lesson - The righteous and faithful prophet will not escape cruel persecution. Isaiah 50:4-9*a*

*Psalm 118:1-2, 19-29

*=As Palm Sunday
**=As Passion Sunday

Psalm 31:9-16

Second Lesson - The condescension of the Son of God to become the Son of Man is offered as a prime example of humility. Philippians 2:5-11

*****Gospel** - Christ enters the capital city riding on a colt. Mark 11:1-11

******Gospel** - The last days of Jesus are described in some detail. Mark 14:1–15:47 or Mark 15:1-39, (40-47)

*CALL TO WORSHIP

Leader: The grace of our Lord Jesus Christ be with you all.

People: And also with you.

Leader: Blessed in the name of the Anointed One are all who come.

People: We are blessed in the house of the Lord.

**CALL TO WORSHIP

Leader: The grace of our Lord Jesus Christ be with you all.

People: And also with you.

Leader: If you saw the Crucified One in the street, would you turn quickly away?

People: We would welcome him, saying, "I put my trust in you. You are my God."

*INVOCATION

With little children and the childlike, O God, we say, Hosanna to the Son of David, the Son of Mary, the Son of God. In this house, sanctified by your Spirit, we praise your holy name and ask you to hear our prayers for the sake of your humble and royal Son, Jesus of Nazareth. Amen

**INVOCATION

Heavenly Parent, we are not ashamed to call your crucified Son, our Lord and God. He willingly permitted himself to be identified with us, leaving your glory to accept human ignominy and suffering with us and for us. Your Holy Spirit inspires our trust. Receive our worship for Jesus' sake. Amen

*PRAYER OF CONFESSION

God of covenants, old and new, carved in stone and written in heart, we confess that we have broken our agreements with you as with others and need your forgiveness for our wrongdoing. Forget our sins and continue your patience with us. We avoid learning because it often entails suffering, and to avoid suffering we seek the way of ease, forgetting that even Jesus learned by the things that he suffered. Forgive us, we pray in his saving name. Amen

**PRAYER OF CONFESSION

All-seeing God, all-loving God, all-encompassing God, we confess that we can ignore what we see, that we can be indifferent to what is too painful to acknowledge, that we can push aside what intrudes on our personal comfort. Forgive such self-centeredness, our lack of compassion, our lack of involvement. Pardon our reluctant and partial imitation of the suffering servanthood of Jesus Christ. Amen

*Declaration of Pardon

Pastor: Friends, hear the good news! Jesus is the source of eternal salvation for all who obey him.

People: Jesus Christ is our Savior.

Pastor: Friends, believe the good news!

People: In Jesus Christ, we are forgiven.

**Declaration of Pardon

Pastor: Friends, hear the good news! The curtain of the Temple was torn in two from top to bottom

People: signifying our ready access to the mercy seat of God.

Pastor: Friends, believe the good news!

People: In Jesus Christ, we are forgiven.

*EXHORTATION

Learn obedience and gain maturity by humble submission in prayer to the will of God.

**EXHORTATION

Be humble in your attitude toward one another and in that way show that your life is like that of our humble Savior, Christ Jesus.

*PRAYER OF THE DAY

Patient Teacher, when we are stubborn as mules, show us a docile donkey, so that when we are willing to bear the burden you place on us, we may find ourselves bearing the Christ. Amen

**PRAYER OF THE DAY

Crucified One, we need your humble spirit if we are to face the ridicule of the unbelieving without retaliation and accept persecution with resignation. So empty us of pride and we will be more like you. Amen

*PRAYER OF THANKSGIVING

We praise you, O God, for the One who comes in your name. We hail the humble Sovereign who comes in the nobility of servanthood and suffering rather than in pomp and circumstance. We welcome the coming reign of the gentle Giant who blesses children, but conquers evil as our champion. Hallowed be the name of Jesus, your anointed One, and the One we choose to follow. Glory to God in the highest. Glory to God in the lowest. Glory to the Spirit who lives in us. Amen

**PRAYER OF THANKSGIVING

What a stake you have struck into the earth, O God! What a gruesome but gracious tree you have planted on Calvary! How can we find the words to express our thanksgiving for the gush of life that flows from the death of your crucified Son? The hallowed symbol of the Cross and the bread and cup of the Table of the new covenant will be our sacrament to the end of time and the everlasting feast of eternity! Amen

*PRAYER OF DEDICATION

Eternal One, though our gifts may wither like palms, and our persons age and grow weak, receive what we give to you in money and in service, and accomplish what will survive with us in eternity. Amen

**PRAYER OF DEDICATION

All the earnings of my lifetime, magnanimous God, are miniscule beside the offering of your Bethlehem Child and Calvary Son, so may I offer myself, my lifetime, my eternity in worship and servanthood. Amen

*/**PRAYERS OF INTERCESSION AND COMMEMORATION

God of creation and cross, Christ of mortality and immortality, Spirit of communication and communion, we call on you to re-create the world that has suffered the ravages of nature and humanity.

We pray for the church that we may be the saving community of your people, preaching the good news, healing the sick, leading the blind, finding the lost, welcoming strangers into your family.

Spirit of truth, free minds enslaved by falsehood and self-deception. Bless all who teach and all who learn, that your wisdom may be appreciated and what is within human reach understood.

Ruler of the world, governor of governments, rule and overrule in the affairs of state, that corruption may be banished, that injustice may be put right, that prejudice may be exposed.

Healer of the sick, grant your touch to all who are sick or injured. Use our hospitals and nursing homes to care for the aged with compassion.

As today we celebrate the triumphal entry of Jesus into Jerusalem—the place of suffering, but ultimate victory—so we rejoice in the vision of John, who saw in heaven a great multitude that no one could count, from every nation, from all tribes and peoples and languages, standing before the throne and before the Lamb, robed in white, with palm branches in their hands. For those known and dear to us who are already in that company we give thanks. That we may be worthy to join in that eternal celebration, we welcome the grace of our Lord Jesus Christ. "Worthy is the Lamb that was slain to receive power and wealth and wisdom and might and honor and glory and blessing!" Amen

Easter

Easter

First Lesson - Here is an early outline of Peter's sermon, the heart of the gospel, which will be preached to the ends of the earth. Acts 10:34-43

[OR]

The prophet foresees the day when God will finally destroy the power of death. Isaiah 25:6-9

Psalm 118:1-2, 14-24

Second Lesson - The apostle Paul reminds the church that the resurrection story is history that can be substantiated by many witnesses. 1 Corinthians 15:1-11

[OR]

Acts 10:34-43

Gospel - The dearest friends of Jesus discover the empty tomb and Mary Magdalene actually meets the Risen Christ. John 20:1-18

CALL TO WORSHIP

Leader: The grace of our Lord Jesus Christ be with you all.

People: And also with you.

Leader: This is the day on which the Lord has acted: let us exult and rejoice in it.

People: We shall not die, but live to proclaim the works of the Lord.

INVOCATION

God undying, Risen Lord, Eternal Spirit, hear our prayers of adoration and our exultation in the victory of Christ over death. On this first day of the week and on every day may we live in the joy that we shall not die, but live to proclaim your wonderful works forever. Amen

PRAYER OF CONFESSION

God of the Sabbath rest, God of Easter Sunday, God of every day, hear our confession. Fear often closes our mouths so that we say nothing to anybody. We are often reluctant to share unusual experiences that doubters will question and cast aspersions on our sanity. Death mystifies us, but to be a witness of a resurrection would dumbfound us also. There is something fearsome about death and grievous in the separation it brings between the living and the dead. We want to overcome our doubts about resurrection. Help us to receive the witness of the apostles concerning the new creation begun after the Sabbath was ended and another first day of your activity began, for the sake of him you raised from death, Jesus Christ. Amen

Declaration of Pardon

Pastor:　Friends, hear the good news! Christ died for our sins in accordance with the Scriptures, was buried, and was raised on the third day in accordance with the Scriptures.

People:　Through this good news we are being saved, if we hold firmly to the message.

Pastor:　Friends, believe the good news!

People:　In Jesus Christ, we are forgiven.

[AND]

Exhortation

Like the apostles and as an apostle, continue to spread the good news of the death and resurrection of our Savior and Lord, Jesus Christ.

PRAYER OF THE DAY

Jesus of Nazareth, crucified mortal, resurrected Christ, send us also from east to west and from north to south, in whatever direction pleases you, with voices filled with the joy of faith and the message of eternal salvation from your cross and empty tomb, that others may share our Easter surprise and not be afraid of death. Amen

PRAYER OF THANKSGIVING

Giver of banquets, dryer of tears, mover of stones, we love your feast of bread and wine, because it is to us the promise of life forever. We know how rare is the wine you make in the winepress of the Cross, and from what wheat is stone-ground the bread of life. All thanks and praise be given to you, for you give us yourself. You have made your salvation known to us in Jesus of Nazareth, crucified and risen from the dead. You move the stone of death from the tomb of Jesus and with it the pall that shrouds every coffin. You will deliver us from the power of death and yet with gentleness wipe away the tears of our partings. Who can compare to you, in generosity, in gentleness, in generating and regenerating life? Alleluia! Amen!

PRAYER OF DEDICATION

Whatever we bring, O God, our hands are basically empty and held out to receive the bounties of your grace. What we bring we give to share with others and to return with them to your Table in thanksgiving here and now, and hereafter in eternity; through Jesus Christ, our risen Lord. Amen

PRAYERS OF INTERCESSION
AND COMMEMORATION

God of the living, Victor over sin and death, living Spirit, give your church victory over doubt that hearing and believing your word, we may be obedient to what you command us to do.

We pray for all world leaders that they may do justice and so honor you, as well as serve the people for whom they bear some responsibility.

We pray for all who doubt, that they may not be content to live with their questions without actively searching for evidences of your love in Christ and the church. We pray for all who are sick and suffering that the victory of Christ over suffering and death may give them new hope of recovery or eternal life, that they may know that in life and in death they are yours.

Eternal God, we remember with thanksgiving those who have loved and served you in your church on earth, who now rest from their labors, especially those most dear to us, whom we name in our hearts before you. Keep us in communion with all your saints, and bring us at last to the joy of your heavenly kingdom. Amen

Second Sunday of Easter

First Lesson - The early Christian community shares all they have so that none are in need. Acts 4:32-35

Psalm 133

Second Lesson - John emphasizes that continuing forgiveness is needed and offered to sustain our relationship with God. 1 John 1:1–2:2

Gospel - A second appearance of the Risen Christ is needed to convince Thomas that Jesus is indeed alive from the dead. John 20:19-31

CALL TO WORSHIP

Leader: The grace of our Lord Jesus Christ be with you all.

People: **And also with you.**

Leader: Hear and read what is written down in the Gospel of John in order that you may believe that Jesus is the Messiah,

People: Jesus Christ is the son of God and through our faith in him we have life.

INVOCATION

Life-giving God, we worship you in hope of everlasting life, because we have heard and believed the good news of Jesus Christ, your Son. Make real to us again the significance of his self-offering and your acceptance of his sacrifice for the salvation of all sinners who, inspired by the Spirit, believe in him. Amen

PRAYER OF CONFESSION

God of all worlds, Easter Victor, Victorious Spirit, though we are declared to be victors over the godless world, we often feel doubtful and defeated. We are too prone to go by our feelings and not to accept the witness of the apostles, believing his victory to be our victory over sin and death. Victorious Spirit, overcome our doubts and fears as we read and hear the apostolic witness. Increase our love as well, for we need to love others who are not as lovable as Jesus Christ. Amen

Declaration of Pardon

Pastor: Friends, hear the good news! The victory that defeats the world is our faith.

People: We are victors over evil by believing that Jesus is the Son of God.

Pastor: Friends, believe the good news!

People: In Jesus Christ, we are forgiven.

[AND]

Exhortation

Obey the commands of the God you love and you will love God's children too.

PRAYER OF THE DAY

God of earth and heaven, Christ of the cross and resurrection, Spirit of creation and re-creation, grant us the blessing you promise to those who believe in the Risen Christ, without visible and tangible proof of his victory over death. Amen

PRAYER OF THANKSGIVING

God of the living, Conqueror of death, Spirit of Love, we give thanks and praise for every victory you give us over our fears, our failures, our selfishness; for the courage to do what would otherwise be impossible for us; and for the companionship of those who work with us in common enterprises. We are grateful for the examples of those who have gone before us, who have given us noble experiments in unselfish service and modeled the selflessness we do not often practice. We praise your giving, your living, your loving, God above us, God beside us, God within us. Amen

PRAYER OF DEDICATION

Living, loving, giving Spirit, surprise us with the joy of living, that overcomes any pain in parting with our money, or pride in giving ourselves. Amen

PRAYERS OF INTERCESSION
AND COMMEMORATION

God of all deeps and all high places, be present to us in our low days and our days of exaltation. Hear our prayers for those who are now experiencing letdown and fatigue, who are trying to regather their energies and regain their perspective on life, who are looking for new directions and true goals.

Guide those who are at the peak of their powers, that their energies and gifts may not be dissipated with what is cheap and self-serving, but expended in what is helpful to others and the expression of their highest creativity.

Govern in the affairs of governments. Bring to fruition the best that governments can do in obedience to your will. Bring to naught the schemes of unprincipled people who use power for its own sake and not for the common good.

There is diversity, as well as a deeper unity, in your church. Help us to find truth in dialogue and in questions by persons in differing positions, so that we're able to share our discoveries with honesty and humility. Teach us how to learn as well as how to teach, how to listen as well as how to speak, when to be still and when it is time to move on.

Heal the sick. Comfort the sad. Prod the lazy. Quiet the overzealous. Rest the weary. Strengthen the weak. Give hope to the despairing.

We rejoice in our fellowship with you, God our Father, and with your Son Jesus Christ. We give thanks for the word of life revealed to us by the Holy Spirit and for the communion we have with you while we walk in its light. We remember with gratitude our communion with others of like precious faith, who have died and entered into your closer company. Make our joy complete when our earthly life is over and we are received into greater glory, through Jesus Christ. To you, Fatherly, Brotherly, Motherly God, be ascribed all glory and light and no darkness at all. Amen

Third Sunday of Easter

First Lesson - Peter boldly witnesses to the resurrection of Jesus to bring those responsible for his death to repentance and new life. Acts 3:12-19

Psalm 4

Second Lesson - John writes of God's love for children not yet perfect and in the process of purification. 1 John 3:1-7

Gospel - The Risen Christ appears to the disciples telling them of the fulfillment of the Scriptures in all that has occurred. Luke 24:36*b*-48

CALL TO WORSHIP

Leader: The grace of our Lord Jesus Christ be with you all.

People: And also with you.

Leader: God is here and everywhere. Pause here to be recharged with the power from above.

People: We will receive God's promised gift.

INVOCATION

God of might and right, we come to worship you, in need of spiritual reenergizing so that we may serve you now and in every opportunity that will come to us. Strengthen us in all good works; through Jesus Christ our Lord. Amen

PRAYER OF CONFESSION

God of all pilgrims, of all children of the faithful, of all wrestlers with the truth, we confess our complicity with many of the evils of society as well as our repentance of some of them in the strength you have given us in the church. We are of the same humanity that repudiated the suffering Messiah. We are of the repenting community whose sins are wiped out. We need to know you more truly so that your divine love may come to perfection in us, through the Spirit of the Risen Christ. Amen

Declaration of Pardon

Pastor: Friends, hear the good news! We have come to plead our cause with the Divine Parent, Jesus Christ, God's Son.

People: Jesus Christ is just and the remedy for the defilement of our sins, and not our sin only but the sins of all the world.

Pastor: Friends, believe the good news!

People: In Jesus Christ, we are forgiven.

[AND]

Exhortation

Bind yourself to love as Christ loved.

PRAYER OF THE DAY

Self-giving God, continue to give us your promised gift that we may be empowered to obey your commands and be faithful proclaimers of the forgiveness of sins to all nations, through the dying and rising Messiah, and his gift with the Father of the Spirit of Love. Amen

PRAYER OF THANKSGIVING

God above us, leading us to exaltation; God beneath us, lifting us out of degradation; God around us, attracting our adoration; God before us, leading us to perfection; God behind us, guarding us from discouragement. Where would we be without you? What future could we anticipate without your leading? We worship you, God of all nations. We follow you, loving Messiah. We welcome you, indwelling Spirit. Amen

PRAYER OF DEDICATION

Risen Christ, give us faith to see that it is into your hands we offer our gifts and that it is your feet we follow when we go out to serve others in the Spirit of love. Amen

PRAYERS OF INTERCESSION
AND COMMEMORATION

Hearing God, Responding Savior, Inspiring Spirit, we offer our prayers as a sign of our faith in you. May we and all the members of the church of Christ cling to your word revealed in the holy Scriptures, seeking also to do what you direct us to do through the commandments and examples of faith that we discover in its pages. May we be faithful in our witness to your love, so that those who suffer doubt may believe and reach out to touch you for whatever they need.

Grant that those who are undergoing trials of sickness and suffering may know your presence and a measure of resignation or healing.

Creator God, you made all things in your wisdom, and in your love you save us. We pray for the whole creation. Confront both godless and believing world leaders with your call to justice and peace. Order unruly powers, deal with injustice. Teach us effective ways to challenge injustice and evil in the power of your Spirit, and with humility, acknowledging our own faults and failings.

God of patriarchs and matriarchs, you are the God of the living, not of the dead. Through your glorified Son, whom you raised from death, you have offered us repentance and forgiveness of sins and eternal life. We rejoice in the promise that because he lives we too shall live. We celebrate with joy the passing over to you of those who lived in such faith and have preceded us into the place you have gone to prepare for us, Living Lord. Holy Spirit, keep us in your communion that we may at the last be together with all the saints in glory everlasting. Amen

Fourth Sunday of Easter

First Lesson - Peter in his preaching identifies Jesus, raised from the dead, as the rejected stone recovered to be the cornerstone of the church. Acts 4:5-12

Psalm 23

Second Lesson - John writes of love made real in truth and in action. 1 John 3:16-24

Gospel - Jesus identifies himself as a good shepherd who gives his life for the salvation of his flock. John 10:11-18

CALL TO WORSHIP

Leader: The grace of our Lord Jesus Christ be with you all.

People: And also with you.

Leader: Approach God with confidence.

People: We will do what God approves and ask what we will.

INVOCATION

Risk-taking God, you have given us a measure of freedom so that we may worship you without coercion. Though we have chosen to be here today, we can not approach you worthily except by the preparation of your Holy Spirit. Receive us for the sake of Jesus Christ, our Redeemer. Amen

PRAYER OF CONFESSION

Creator, Repairer, Sustainer of consciences, we need your continued attention, because at times our consciences are dull or numb and need to be set true again, and sensitive to what should bother us. Confrontation of painful truth may be what we need to jolt us into action that is appropriate for the children of God. Forgive our avoidance of what we should do and our neglect of what we started but have not finished, for the sake of Jesus, who finished what you sent him to do. Amen

Declaration of Pardon

Pastor: Friends, hear the good news! Jesus, our Good Shepherd, laid down his life for us, his sheep.

People: Jesus laid down his life for us that we might live.

Pastor: Friends, believe the good news!

People: In Jesus Christ, we are forgiven.

[AND]

Exhortation

Give allegiance to God's Son, Jesus Christ, and love one another as he commanded.

PRAYER OF THE DAY

Good Shepherd, hasten the day when it will be clear that there is one flock and one shepherd, when above all the discordant voices of our times, your voice will be heard loud and clear. Amen

PRAYER OF THANKSGIVING

Bountiful Host, what a profusion of good things you have created for us to enjoy. Your provisions for the sustenance of the body and the spirit are beyond measure, our cup overflows. Your promises are sure and we expect your goodness and mercy to nurture us all our days and bring us to the time and place where we know your presence even more intimately than today. Today and every day, may we remember to express our thanksgiving. Amen

PRAYER OF DEDICATION

Actions are what you look for, Bishop of the church, so let these words and these offerings signify what we will do to serve you. Amen

PRAYERS OF INTERCESSION AND COMMEMORATION

With all our heart and with all our mind,
let us pray to the Lord, saying,
"Lord, hear our prayer."
For the peace of the world,
for the welfare of the church of God,
and for the unity of all people,
let us pray to the Lord.
Lord, hear our prayer.
For our national leader,
for the leaders of the nations,
and for all in authority,
let us pray to the Lord.
Lord, hear our prayer.
For those who are poor and oppressed,
for those unemployed and destitute,
for prisoners and captives,
and for all who remember and care for them,
let us pray to the Lord.
Lord, hear our prayer.
Mighty God: in Jesus Christ you dealt with spirits that darken minds or set people against themselves and others. Give peace to people who are torn by conflict, are cast down or dream deceiving dreams. By your power, drive from our mind demons that shake confidence and wreck love. Tame unruly forces in us, and bring us to your truth, so that we may accept ourselves as good, glad children of your love, known in Jesus Christ.
We pray that all may go well with our family and friends and that they may be in good health, both physically and

spiritually. Restore those who are sick in body, mind, or spirit.

Eternal God, we rejoice with those who have received their desire to depart and be with Christ, for that better life without sin and suffering. Bring us in your own time to the passage from life through death to that better life in sure and certain faith in the living Christ who promises to be with us always. And to you, Fatherly, Brotherly, Motherly God, be given all esteem and love by all your children in earth and heaven. Amen

Fifth Sunday of Easter

First Lesson - Philip baptizes the Ethiopian eunuch after his conversion. Acts 8:26-40

Psalm 22:25-31

Second Lesson - John writes that love should have a human dimension as an extension of the love God has for us. 1 John 4:7-21

Gospel - Jesus describes our connection with him as branches on the vine. John 15:1-8

CALL TO WORSHIP

Leader: The grace of our Lord Jesus Christ be with you all.

People: And also with you.

Leader: Seek the Sovereign of all nations.

People: We will praise God and be in good heart forever.

INVOCATION

Your Spirit, O God, brings us in good and cheerful heart to worship you humbly with more reverence than is due any earthly sovereign or leader. May our worship be a renewed commitment to daily service of your cause; through Jesus Christ our Lord. Amen

PRAYER OF CONFESSION

Divine Gardener, you have planted the true Vine in our world and sustain living branches by the Spirit. We confess that we do not always readily receive into our fellowship those you send to us. We are suspicious of those who seem different or whose sincerity we question. We may fear that we will be replaced, forgetting that you want your church to grow like a healthy vineyard, well-pruned of dead wood and producing the fruits of the Spirit. Forgive us if we, in pride, seek to take over your role as Gardener, discontent to be but branches of your true vine, Jesus Christ. Amen

Declaration of Pardon

Pastor: Friends, hear the good news! God is love, and God's love was disclosed to us in the sending of the divine Son into the world to bring us life.

People: The divine Son, Jesus Christ, is the remedy of the defilement of our sins.

Pastor: Friends, believe the good news!

People: In Jesus Christ, we are forgiven.

[AND]

Exhortation

Remain united with the Vine, Jesus Christ. No branch can bear fruit by itself.

PRAYER OF THE DAY

Divine Vine Tender, so prune and tie us as branches of the vine that, being rid of all unfruitfulness and directed by the commands of Christ, we may bear fruit to your glory and our joy. Amen

PRAYER OF THANKSGIVING

God of all nations, Universal Christ, Including Spirit, we praise your name and names for the love that embraces us and the ties that bind us together as a church across all lines of race and class, across the centuries from the beginning until now, across all stages of human growth from childhood to old age. Our baptism, by whatever mode, has joined us to you in a living relationship that spans all human differences and will survive beyond the grave. We give you hearty thanks and unceasing praise, for your love is beyond all imagining. Amen

PRAYER OF DEDICATION

Giving God, receive what we give to you in response to the loving gift of Jesus, your divine Child, so that we may be assured that you know of our love for you however small in comparison with your gifts to us. Amen

PRAYERS OF INTERCESSION
AND COMMEMORATION

God of earth and heaven, hear our prayers for the world that you have loved with an unforgetting, giving love. Bring to mind those who are often forgotten, those who are the last of their generation, those who are the only one in their family, those who are bereft of the one to whom they were most dear and who were most dear to them. Lead us to such lonely ones that we may include them in our families.

Monarch of all nations and peoples, acknowledged and

ignored, call all nations to give the tribute of worship to your oneness that the broken and hostile factions of humanity may find unity in your worship and peace with justice.

Epitome of Parenthood and Parent of all parents, help both parents and children to find ways of communicating openly and honestly, both hearing and being heard, so that there may be agreement that will give to each the maximum of both freedom and responsibility.

Creator of the perfect and Healer of the imperfect, grant a continuance in health to those who are well and healing and recovery to those who are sick. Hear us as we name in our hearts those whose illness and injury are on our minds.

Continue to provide gifts of healing to your church that as the apostles healed in the name of Jesus Christ of Nazareth so today also the lame will walk and deaf hear and the mute speak to give praise to your holy name. In the congregation may the sick call for the elders of the church and have them pray over them, anointing them with oil in the name of the Lord. So may the prayer of faith save the sick, the Lord raise them up; and anyone who has committed sins be forgiven.

God of all times and places, we praise you for all your servants who having been faithful to you on earth, now live with you in heaven. Keep us in communion with them until we meet with all your children in the joy of your eternal kingdom; through Jesus Christ our Lord. Amen

Sixth Sunday of Easter

First Lesson - Jewish Christians who came with Peter are surprised when the gift of the Holy Spirit is given to

Gentile believers. Acts 10:44-48

Psalm 98

Second Lesson - Love of the heavenly parent should include family love for all God's children. 1 John 5:1-6

Gospel - The disciples of Jesus are called to the intimacy of friendship from the relationship of master/servant. John 15:9-17

CALL TO WORSHIP

Leader: The grace of our Lord Jesus Christ be with you all.

People: **And also with you.**

Leader: Sing praises in God's honor with the harp and the music of the psaltery.

People: **With musical instruments we acclaim the presence of God, our Sovereign.**

INVOCATION

With musical instruments as well as our variety of voices, we worship you, O God, for you rule the world. May we deepen our loyalties to you in this time of reflection as we hear your word in the book and by the Spirit of Jesus Christ. Amen

PRAYER OF CONFESSION

God without favorites, from every nation you accept the person who reveres you and does what is right, but we do what is unacceptable to you. We need the forgiveness and spiritual healing that you offer us in Jesus of Nazareth and the Holy Spirit. Free us from the oppression of evil that we may be free to worship you with great joy and, bearing witness to Christ crucified and raised from the dead, may see the baptism of others who put their trust in his name. Amen

Declaration of Pardon

Pastor: Friends, hear the good news! You are of God's family.

People: The One inspiring us is greater than the evil spirit inspiring the godless world.

Pastor: Friends, believe the good news!

People: In Jesus Christ, we are forgiven.

[AND]

Exhortation

Do not trust any and every spirit in the world, for there are many prophets falsely inspired and not from God, and do not acknowledge that Jesus Christ has come in humanity from God.

PRAYER OF THE DAY

Loving Parent, commanding Presence, keep us in your love so that in humble acceptance of our election we may accomplish our appointed task in the freedom of friendship rather than the duty of servitude, loving and serving as Jesus did. Amen

PRAYER OF THANKSGIVING

For all judges who are committed to justice as you are, O God, we give you thanks, trusting in the final victory of goodness. For all prophets who are inspired by your Spirit of truth, anointed One, intent on being faithful witnesses to you, we praise your name, Jesus of Nazareth. For all musicians, who, receiving your Spirit, Universal One, celebrate the beauty of creation, the baptism of your grace, the unity of your church, we express our gratitude and join them as we can, with voices and instruments of all kinds. We worship you with all kindred souls in every time and place with humility and love and obedience. Amen

PRAYER OF DEDICATION

We serve you, Great God, with whatever we have, with our financial resources, with our musical skills, with our voices and our pens, with hands that can be folded in prayer and open in the service of others, with our feet that bring us here and take us out again into the world for which you gave your Son Jesus in life and resurrection. Amen

PRAYERS OF INTERCESSION
AND COMMEMORATION
(May be used for Mother's Day)

Mother of us all, Father of us all, Brother of us all, hear our prayer for the whole human family. We need your good grace in the whole human race, so we can play international games without spite and without racial and political name-calling and hostility. May international sports teach fair play and high performance without cheating and violence. Send us universal mothers who know how to pacify squabbling children, teaching them to play fairly and to share their toys, to forgive and forget, patiently producing another generation that will refuse to make war and will invent new games, that will play exotic music to dance with the bounding beauty of the deer in the forests.

Teach us to sing in new harmonies that will transpose all the grating sounds of our times into the hallelujahs of heaven. Let the world's servants hear again the words of Mary concerning her son, Jesus, "whatever he tells you to do, do it." So may your will be done on earth as it is in heaven.

We pray that all may go well with our mothers today and that they may be in good health physically and spiritually. We give thanks for mothers in Israel like Deborah and in the church like Mary, mother of our Lord.

We remember with thanksgiving all our mothers, living and dead, who were a source of life and grace to us in our birth and in our growing up. We celebrate your eternal rest for mothers whose work was never done and whose love had no limits. Grant us at the last to be united with them in your heavenly home with all whom we have loved and lost awhile.

To your name Fatherly, Brotherly, Motherly God, we ascribe all majesty and perfection and love. Amen

Seventh Sunday of Easter

First Lesson - Spiritual transformation, not merely new rituals, are what the Eternal One desires from God's people. Acts 1:15-17, 21-26

Psalm 1

Second Lesson - The greatest affirmative action in history is the sending of Jesus as the confirmation of God's gracious promises. 1 John 5:9-13

Gospel - Only God has the final authority to forgive our sins and that authority was shared with the Son of Man, Jesus of Nazareth. John 17:6-19

CALL TO WORSHIP

Leader: The grace of our Lord Jesus Christ be with you all.

People: And also with you.

Leader: Christ has gone up with shouts of acclamation to the right hand of the throne of the eternal.

People: We acclaim our God with shouts of joy, and praise our Monarch and Prince with psalms and fanfares.

INVOCATION

God most high, Christ at your right hand, your Spirit within us inspires our praise with psalms and musical offerings of acclamation. Hear our petitions also as our advocate Jesus Christ presents them to you in his name. Amen

PRAYER OF CONFESSION

God invisible in majesty, God incognito in the world, name-sharing God, how could we know you more fully than as you have revealed yourself in the One who came into the world but has ascended again into the holiest place? We need to be consecrated by the truth, since we are too ready to compromise it rather than be treated as strange, as Jesus often was. Forgive us if we have been ashamed to confess the name of Christ and denied the power of that name to cleanse us from the defilement of sin and to keep us from further exposure to the evil one who would lead us astray. Deliver us from evil through the power of the Spirit imparted to us in Christ's name. Amen

Declaration of Pardon

Pastor: Friends, hear the good news! God loved us by sending his Son as the remedy for the defilement of our sins.

People: We receive God's Son as the remedy for the defilement of our sins.

Pastor: Friends, believe the good news!

People: In Jesus Christ, we are forgiven.

[AND]

Exhortation

If God thus loved us, dear friends, we in turn are bound to love one another.

PRAYER OF THE DAY

Holy and powerful Parent, while we are still in the world, remind us of the power of the name you share with us through Jesus Christ, so that, truly honoring that name by our behavior, we may be kept from the evil one and come at last to your presence, no stranger to your love and grace. Amen

PRAYER OF THANKSGIVING

God, loving and inseparable; Son of God, loving and send-able; Spirit of God, loving and impartable; we have come to know and believe the love that you have for us. We are grateful for the love we share in the family of Jesus Christ, as his brothers and sisters. Your love is being brought to perfection within us through our need to seek and grant forgiveness, through our search for the full and true meaning of your Word, in the struggle to understand one another and overcome misunderstanding. For all experiences of growth and every increased capacity to love as you love, we express our thanksgiving. For every discovery of new kinship in the Spirit, we rejoice with great joy, as your family continues to grow locally and internationally. All praise to you, all-loving God. Amen

PRAYER OF DEDICATION

Eternal Parent, as you sent your Son into the world to show your love, send us also from this place to where our witness to the truth will also be an expression of your love, through Jesus Christ our Savior. Amen

PRAYERS OF INTERCESSION
AND COMMEMORATION

Distant God, Ascended Christ, Descended Spirit, you bridge cosmic and planetary distances. Encourage us to make the acquaintance of those who are in our neighborhoods but who are not in our own circle of friends. In working together for the service of our community, may we find places to use the talents of all. There are conditions elsewhere in our county that we can help meet as we share common social services both tax-supported and volunteer. Enlarge our imagination to develop cooperative projects helpful to all. Increase our sense of the smallness of the world neighborhood that we may share our plenty with those in places of want, whether around the corner or across the ocean. As our planet is encircled by satellites giving us pictures of weather and recording other data for many purposes, give us a vision of the world as it might be without artificial barriers and competing military establishments.

May the true catholicity of the church set an example of openness as we practice cooperation rather than competition in the sharing of the good news of Jesus, knowing that only as outsiders enter the church and become part of it, does the church grow.

Hear our prayers for all who search for new cures for disease and surgical techniques to remedy birth defects. Bless nurses and doctors who minister to our sick and care for the aged in hospitals and nursing homes. Especially bless those are in hospices that their dying may be completed with the least suffering and with spiritual comfort from chaplains and staff.

Heavenly Father, we believe that you have granted the desire of your Holy Son Jesus, that those whom you have given him should be with him where he now is. We rejoice for those who are beyond our present sight but who see the glory of the ascended Christ, which has been his, with your love, from before the foundation of the world. May your Holy Spirit abide with us as we complete our earthly life and prepare to enjoy your glory as well. To you, Fatherly, Brotherly, Motherly God, One God, be all glory and praise. Amen

Pentecost

First Lesson - The Spirit of God bridges language barriers to begin the creation of one church for Jesus Christ. Acts 2:1-21

[OR]

The visual parable that Ezekiel experiences is a sign of the resurrection of the people of God. Ezekiel 37:1-14

Psalm 104:24-34, 35*b*

Second Lesson - Paul places the new life of the people of God in the context of cosmic reconstruction. Romans 8:22-27

[OR]

Acts 2:1-21

Gospel - Jesus prepares the disciples for further teaching by the Spirit and ongoing guidance in the apostolic ministry. John 15:26-27 and 16:4-15

CALL TO WORSHIP

Leader: The grace of our Lord Jesus Christ be with you all.

People: **And also with you.**

Leader: Look to our Creator who gives breath to all breathing creatures

People: **and the Spirit to all who pray.**

INVOCATION

You bless us doubly, Great God, in giving us life and breath and also the Holy Spirit to inspire our prayers. We open ourselves to the Spirit who will instill in us the wisdom of Jesus Christ and all that you will teach us from your holy word, in his name. Amen

119

PRAYER OF CONFESSION

Unseen Parent, departed Brother, promised Counselor, we admit that we have not always confessed that we have done what is wrong. We do not always seek the truth to know and do what is right. Though we should declare our faults and failing out of sheer love and trust, we more often confess because of the threat of future judgment. Forgive indifference and noncommittal discipleship with too much drift and very little direction. We need the intensity and intentionality of your Son Jesus through the promised Spirit. Amen

Declaration of Pardon

Pastor: Friends, hear the good news! Everyone who invokes Jesus Christ by name shall be saved.

People: Jesus Christ is our Savior.

Pastor: Friends, believe the good news!

People: In Jesus Christ, we are forgiven.

[AND]

Exhortation

Be open to God who will pour out the Spirit on all humanity, so that our children will prophesy, the old will dream dreams, and the young see visions.

PRAYER OF THE DAY

Spirit of truth, guide us into all truth, so that we may know where wrong and right and judgment lie, and in knowing what is coming, stand with you and not with the Prince of this world, who already stands condemned. Amen

PRAYER OF THANKSGIVING

Doer-of-great-things, glorified Truth-teller, truthful Advocate, what great things you do, and promise, and fulfill.

We are continually amazed at the speech you give the speechless, the power you give to the powerless, the meaning you give to those whose lives have seemed meaningless. We live in anticipation of what your loving Spirit can still do as people are open to the gifts your Spirit will give in and through the church of Jesus Christ. We glorify you, Father, Son, and mothering Spirit. Amen

PRAYER OF DEDICATION

You, too, are Mind, and Body, and Spirit, O God. We bring our offerings to support the church's ministry of learning and doing and praying to the glory of your name. Amen

PRAYER OF INTERCESSION AND COMMEMORATION

God transcending, descending, condescending; Our God, though nothing escapes your attention, we are putting ourselves "on line" with you, wanting to be part of your network of accessible love and benefaction. Free from greed and irresponsibility international agencies that could find new ways of bridging cultural, political, and economic differences between nations so that famine, disease, and homelessness may be eradicated and not just dealt with in crisis times. Continue to inspire your church and its agencies of cooperation that are involved in such concerns in the whole world that it may show governmental agencies what can be done when differences are put aside for the care of those in dire need. Protect those who risk their lives and health in the front lines of the war against hunger and want of every kind. Show us new ways of transcending economic problems that will not deprive some to enrich others and create divisions between people and nations. Help us to do what we can to solve problems of unemployment and poverty in our own neighborhoods, as well as support the mission of the church and international relief agencies.

Hear our prayers for those persons who are looking to us

today for our intercessions. Minister to them as you know they have need.

God of all times and places, we praise you for all your servants who, having been faithful to you on earth, now live with you in heaven. Keep us in communion with them until we meet with all your children in the joy of your eternal kingdom; through Jesus Christ our Lord. Amen

After Pentecost

Trinity Sunday

First Lesson - The prophet's vision of the holiness and glory of God overwhelms him with a sense of unworthiness to be the divine messenger. Isaiah 6:1-8

Psalm 29

Second Lesson - Kinship to God includes the guidance of the Spirit but no exemption from suffering. Romans 8:12-17

Gospel - Nicodemus comes to Jesus by night to learn how spiritual renewal may take place. John 3:1-17

CALL TO WORSHIP

Leader: The grace of our Lord Jesus Christ be with you all.

People: And also with you.

Leader: Search for a vision of God. Listen for the voices of God's messengers.

People: We will search and listen and enlist in the embassy of God.

INVOCATION

Infinite and invisible God, incarnate and human Spokesperson, universal and communicating Spirit, we come to see with the eyes and ears of the heart, so manifest yourself to us again in the Spirit speaking through your Word. Amen

PRAYER OF CONFESSION

Three-times-holy One, our best parenting is but a shadow of your giving and caring for us. Our devotion to brothers and sisters can hardly be compared to the self-giving of Jesus Christ, Our Brother. The most understanding and forgiving family spirit we share is hardly comparable to the unity in love, which is your nature. We are lost if we flee your loving discipline. We are estranged if we deny your Son Jesus. We are orphaned if we are not bound to you by the Spirit. Mercifully keep us in your family through Jesus Christ our Savior. Amen

Declaration of Pardon

Pastor: Friends, hear the good news! You are not obliged to live on the level of your lower nature.

People: All of us who are moved by the Spirit of God are children of God.

Pastor: Friends, believe the good news!

People: In Jesus Christ, we are forgiven.

[AND]

Exhortation

By the Spirit, put to death all the base pursuits of the body, and you will live in the freedom of the children of God.

PRAYER OF THE DAY

Paternal God, Brotherly Christ, Motherly Spirit, help us to see in your gospel the sign of your presence with and work through the Christ, that seeing the evidence of your power, then and now, we may experience a rebirth of the Spirit, enabled to see and enter the place where you alone rule uncontested. Amen

PRAYER OF THANKSGIVING

Glorious God, you fill the universe with majestic beauty and flowers in unexpected places. Holy God, you hallow awesome sanctuaries, humbling us with the sense of our smallness and our sins. Sanctifying Spirit, you purify us, removing our iniquities and renewing us as if childlike in innocence, starting life again. We worship you with songs and verses, new songs and old songs with old instruments and new instruments of music, with processions and dances, with liturgy and daily work. All thanks be given to you for your great gifts of nature and grace, unseen Creator, Firstborn of creation, re-creating Spirit. Amen

PRAYER OF DEDICATION

Understanding Parent, though we rejoice to be joint heirs of splendor with Jesus Christ, is it possible that we lose if we do not give until it hurts? Teach us how to share the sufferings of the Christ, for his name's sake. Amen

PRAYERS OF INTERCESSION AND COMMEMORATION
(May be used for Memorial Day Sunday)

God of our ancestors, God of our own generation and of our children and grandchildren, we pray for our nation on this weekend of remembrance, that we may honor all who have died in the defense of our freedom against tyrannical rulers of every time. Grant that we may continue our vigilance in the preservation of freedom of speech for all whether they agree or disagree with us. May our love of truth and our faith in its power to free, save us from suppression of debate and the lawful expression of dissent.

We pray for those who practice the Christian faith under the dangers of persecution and the pressures of atheistic governments that they may be encouraged in their minority positions and remain true to their convictions. May the good news that you have sent into the world continue to be carried by public media and secret sharing where freedom of religion is denied.

Inspire your people to political activity in democracies, not divorcing their faith from their responsibilities as citizens. Comfort those who have been imprisoned for their convictions in countries with repressive governments.

Bless also those who minister to criminals in our prisons. May the good news bring a change of heart and encouragement to live out that change both inside the bars and outside when they are released.

Hear our prayers for all who are bereaved and adjusting to life without one dear to them. Remember, O God, any whom we have forgotten. Your own Spirit bears witness with our spirit, "Abba! Father!" that we are your children and joint heirs with Christ—if, in fact, we suffer with him so that we may also be glorified with him. We rejoice that you have already taken to glory many of this generation and past generations who confessed their faith in Christ and served him in the church. By the Spirit, put to death the deeds of our sinful bodies, so that we may live, and led by the Spirit be worthy children of God. To you, Father, Son, and Holy Spirit, be ascribed all majesty, dominion, and power, time without end. Amen

Proper 4 (May 29-June 4)

First Lesson - Young Samuel responds to the call of God to serve in succession to Eli. 1 Samuel 3:1-10 (11-20)

Psalm 139:1-6, 13-18

Second Lesson - Extraordinary gifts can be found in human vessels. 2 Corinthians 4:5-12

Gospel - Jesus exercises healing powers and does this work of compassion on the day of rest. Mark 2:23–3:6

CALL TO WORSHIP

Leader: The grace of our Lord Jesus Christ be with you all.

People: **And also with you.**

Leader: Jesus Christ is Lord and the Light of God. Come to the Light.

People: **Come to the light that shines out of darkness.**

INVOCATION

In a dark world we live; from a dark world we come to worship, God of light. We have come to confess that we believe Jesus Christ to be our Lord and Savior. Let your light by the Spirit shine out of us wherever we go. Amen

PRAYER OF CONFESSION

Holy God, devout Christ, sanctifying Spirit, cleanse our speech from any trivial use of your hallowed name. Save us from attributing to you the hatreds and curses that issue from our anger whether justified or not. May our restraint turn others from the blasphemous use of your name and the desecration of what is holy. Hallowed be your name, Father, Son, and Holy Spirit. Amen

Declaration of Pardon

Pastor: Friends, hear the good news! The death that Jesus died in us reveals also the life that Jesus lives.

People: **We die and live again in Christ.**

Pastor: Friends, believe the good news!

People: **In Jesus Christ, we are forgiven.**

[AND]

Exhortation

Keep a day of rest from work for everyone in your household so that you can give thanks to God for freedom and all of God's great gifts.

PRAYER OF THE DAY

Cure us, healing Christ, on this and every day of rest, that being restored in body, mind, and spirit, we may do what is good, learn what is helpful, and return to our daily work invigorated and inspired. Amen

PRAYER OF THANKSGIVING

Creator of light, we rejoice in the sunrise of each day, whether veiled with clouds or brilliant with the colors of morning. We celebrate your glory revealed in the face of Jesus Christ. Whether in the somber light of Good Friday or the bright glory of Resurrection morning, we live in the light your Spirit spreads in our minds and hearts, thankful for new understanding of your purposes for us, for fresh courage to face adversity, for new moral life as our sins are put to death. We praise you, Light above us, Light beside us, Light within us. Amen

PRAYER OF DEDICATION

God of power, you generously share your divine power with us in the plain earthenware that we are as the church of your beloved Son, Jesus. Our offering of time, money, and ourselves is to provide such humble media for the use of your Spirit, in the name of Jesus Christ. Amen

PRAYER OF INTERCESSION
AND COMMEMORATION

God, our loving Parent, remember those who are in any kind of trouble.

Be near to those who have lost loved ones, and who cannot get used to being alone, homes from which a father who was the wage earner and the support of the household, or a mother on whom everything depended, has been taken away.

Mend homes that have been broken, and bring together

again those who have been separated from one another; and in such homes bless children who have been despoiled of the love that was their right to have.

Comfort and heal those in illness and pain, those whose nerves have broken under the tension of living, those whom the kindly light of reason has left, those who in their own foolishness have become the victim of drugs, or of habits that they cannot break, and which are breaking them.

Bless all little children and protect them from predators, that they may grow up in innocence and joy. Help all young people to find the ideals that will protect them from the strong temptations that beset them.

Refresh those in midlife, those who bear the burden and the heat of the day, those who have the responsibility of earning a living and making a home. Help them to go on even when things seem too much for them.

Sustain those who are old, to whom the years brought loneliness, those who feel that no one wants them now. Help them to wait patiently until the long night closes and the new day dawns.

Renew your Church. Reunite its divisions; strengthen witness; make lovely its service to you and neighbors.

Bless our country and world. Raise up for us leaders who put principle before power, who would rather be right than popular, who would rather be used in service than make use of others.

Bless all our loved ones, our absent friends, and help us always to remember that nothing can separate them or us from your love in life or in death. Show your love to each one of us. Be light in darkness, our strength in weakness, our protection in temptation, our refuge in danger, our comfort in sorrow.

Bring us at last with all your faithful people to the life in which there is no more weakness or suffering, temption or sorrow. Be our eternal friend as you are to those who have gone ahead of us to your final glory and peace. All this we ask through Christ our Lord, who with you and the Holy Spirit we honor and praise. Amen.

Proper 5 (June 5-11)

First Lesson - Samuel warns the elders of Israel that there are drawbacks to having a human king. 1 Samuel 8:4-20 (11:14-15)

Psalm 138

Second Lesson - The apostle Paul speaks of a heavenly kingdom beyond death. 2 Corinthians 4:13–5:1

Gospel - The family of God is marked by faith in Jesus and the work he was called to do. Mark 3:20-35

CALL TO WORSHIP

Leader: The grace of our Lord Jesus Christ be with you all.

People: And also with you.

Leader: Let us call upon God most high to fulfill the divine purpose.

People: God most high, send us truth and love that never fails.

INVOCATION

Responsive God, you are awesome but approachable through your Son and our brother, Jesus Christ. May both our worship and our daily behavior be according to your will that we may be true brothers and sisters of the Christ. Amen

PRAYER OF CONFESSION

King Eternal, Prince of Peace, Royal Spirit, teach us to make the distinction between obedience to your will and the laws of human government. We confess that we are too often content to live by human law and not the higher commands of our Lord Jesus Christ. While we seek to be good citizens of the nation where we live, enable us to abide by the even higher standards of your realm of truth and goodness; through Jesus Christ our Lord. Amen

Declaration of Pardon

Pastor: Friends, hear the good news! The One who raised Christ Jesus to life will, with Jesus, raise us too, and bring us to his presence.

People: Because he lives, we too shall live.

Pastor: Friends, believe the good news!

People: In Jesus Christ, we are forgiven.

[AND]

Exhortation

Fix your eyes not on the things that are seen, but on the things that are unseen. What is seen passes away. What is unseen is eternal.

PRAYER OF THE DAY

Creator of all, from Eden to the end of the world, watch over your people of the promise, forgiving our disobedience, that we may drink the new wine with all who trust your grace in Jesus Christ our Savior. Amen

PRAYER OF THANKSGIVING

God of grace, from the old world to the new, from the Atlantic to the Pacific, there is increasing thanksgiving to you as your merciful power raises us from death to life, bridging the gap that has separated us from you, and spanning the gulf between the transient and the eternal. By the Spirit, you are renewing our inner nature every day until we shall be radiant with your glory, in Jesus Christ, our Light and Light of the world. Amen

PRAYER OF DEDICATION

Head of this household, our offerings are an expression of our commitment to do your will and be the brothers and sisters of Jesus Christ. Amen

PRAYERS OF INTERCESSION AND COMMEMORATION

God for all seasons, for frigid winters and boiling summers, for brisk falls and tepid springs, be with us in all the vicissitudes of life. Guide and direct the bursting energies of the young, the liveliness that can be full of fun, but also adventurousness and daring, not only in sports but in moral and spiritual crusades. Grant patience and perseverance to the those whose lives have mellowed and warmed to the needs of the helpless, those who have run aground. Bless those who have reached the fall and who are aware of declining strength and endurance, who still have gifts to give and goals to achieve but need time to reach them. Let those whose days and years are numbered find places of shelter where they can rest and do what they can and find help in what they can no longer do for themselves. Save us from the hazards to the spirit that are a part of every season of our lives, from recklessness, from confusion, from doubt and despair. Give us opportunities to share what we have learned with others and receive in turn the exchange of their experience.

Divine Governor, rule in the affairs of nations that injustice may be rebuked and the just given strength. Temper justice with mercy and mature tolerance to the fullness of love.

Hear our prayers for the sick. Save those whose sins we fear and whose names we hide in our hearts where only you can read them.

We give you thanks, O God, for all who have fought the good fight and finished their race and kept the faith, and for those dear to us who are at rest with you, especially those who have died in the past year. Grant us grace to follow them as they followed Christ. Bring us, with them, to those things that no eye has seen, nor ear heard, which you have prepared for those who love you. To your name, with the church on earth and the church in heaven, we ascribe all honor and glory, forever and ever. Amen

Proper 6 (June 12-18)

First Lesson - Samuel anoints David to be king over Israel after the failure of Saul on the throne. 1 Samuel 15:34–16:13

Psalm 20

Second Lesson - For Paul, the death and resurrection of Jesus is a preparation for his and our salvation. 2 Corinthians 5:6-10, (11-13), 14-17

Gospel - The Gospel according to Mark includes parables that the other Gospels include in more detail. Mark 4:26-34

CALL TO WORSHIP

Leader: The grace of our Lord Jesus Christ be with you all.

People: And also with you.

Leader: Come to Christ, the great storyteller, and he will teach you in public and in private the meaning of life.

People: **We have come to Christ to learn the true meaning of life.**

INVOCATION

God of all wisdom, Truth and Wisdom Incarnate, Spirit of truth and wisdom, we come to hear your word as it is written, and to commune with you in Spirit. Teach us what we need to know and inspire us for what we ought to do; through Jesus Christ our Lord. Amen

PRAYER OF CONFESSION

God of here and there, Judge of now and then, though you are beyond our line of sight and we must walk by faith, we believe that you are always aware of us and what we do. We know we are on trial, being tested, our conduct under your scrutiny. We confess that our behavior is neither as good nor as bad as it might be. We are not as ambitious for your acceptance as we might be. As exiles, we are anxious to leave the testing grounds behind us, to live with you beyond all danger of failure. Forgive all badness for the sake of Jesus Christ and the goodness he shares with us. Amen

Declaration of Pardon

Pastor: Friends, hear the good news! Those who are planted in the house of the Lord will flourish in the courts of our God.

People: **We are eager to declare that the Lord is just in whom there is no unrighteousness.**

Pastor: Friends, believe the good news!

People: **In Jesus Christ, we are forgiven.**

[AND]

Exhortation

Never cease to be confident, that when we leave our home in the body that we will go to live with the Lord. Live now to be acceptable to the Christ in all you do.

PRAYER OF THE DAY

Public Teacher, private Tutor, increase our ability to receive all that you teach, so that as your disciples we may be able to understand all that you will explain and follow you wherever you lead. Amen

PRAYER OF THANKSGIVING

Sovereign Forester, you cut down the proud tree to leave room for the hidden tree to grow, You nurture the seedling and give life again to the tree that appears to be dead. Your wisdom is beyond our understanding. You bring goodness to maturity in the most unlikely places and in most mysterious ways. Who could believe that your church could grow from twelve to five hundred and from thousands to millions? That your rule should spread from Palestine to the ends of the earth? We are thankful that your realm grows in depth and ever-extending sweep, and that the end of history, as its beginning, is in your hands. All praise to you, Planter and Reaper, God of yesterday and tomorrow. Christ of our youth and our old age, unfailing Spirit of Life. Amen

PRAYER OF DEDICATION

God of all living things, landscape your world with the spreading shrubs and trees of your church that all things beautiful and good may flourish and add glory to your name. Amen

PRAYERS OF INTERCESSION
AND COMMEMORATION

Father, for whom all fathers are named; Son, like whom all sons and daughters should be; Spirit, by whom all families should be gathered close in Christian love; hear our prayers for all families, those who are part of this church family and those who live around us.

Bless those families recently bereaved who are needing to form new ways of relating and compensating for the loss of the one recently deceased. Guide those families who need to make adjustments in their relationships with children and the larger family because of separation and divorce.

Strengthen families threatened by the serious illness of a member of their family and whose recovery is uncertain. Let their hope be in you who are ours in life and death.

Remind the nations of their common humanity, that they are not self-created, but that all life comes from you, and that we are accountable to you for what we do with our time on earth. Save us from blind hatred and wild vengeance that so often injure and kill the most innocent.

God of all times and places, we praise you for all your servants who, having been faithful to you on earth, now live with you in heaven. Keep us in communion with them until we meet with all your children in the joy of your eternal kingdom; through Jesus Christ our Lord. Amen

Proper 7 (June 19-25)

First Lesson - David and Goliath fight as champions for the Israelites and the Philistines. 1 Samuel 17:(1*a*, 4-11, 19-23), 32-49

Psalm 9:9-20

[OR]

After David's victory over Goliath, Saul and Jonathan treat him as a prince and take him to the palace. 1 Samuel 17:57–18:5

[AND]

Psalm 133

Second Lesson - The apostle Paul outlines some of the difficulties faced in his ministry and the resources brought to bear in dealing with them. 2 Corinthians 6:1-13

Gospel - Jesus has quite different power than his human ancestor King David. Mark 4:35-41

CALL TO WORSHIP

Leader: The grace of our Lord Jesus Christ be with you all.

People: And also with you.

Leader: God's name deserves our praise in this house.

People: God's name deserves our praise to the farthest bounds of the earth.

INVOCATION

Hallowed be your name, O God, by our prayers and our hymns as we are gathered to worship you. Hallowed be your name, O Christ, in this house of prayer and in our homes and schools and wherever we live and work. Hallowing Spirit, purify our minds and our mouths to the glory of God. Amen

PRAYER OF CONFESSION

Creator of the good, Recoverer of the good, Inspirer of the good, our grandest cities and our finest houses are at best pale shadows of the city of God. We have corrupted them with vice and violence and greed. We have only belatedly made more adequate provision for the handicapped.

Forgive our failures in making our highest dreams come true, with the strength of justice, the humanity of compassion, the dignity of equality. It is not the city of this world but the City of Christ that we need. Amen

Declaration of Pardon

Pastor: Friends, hear the good news! God was in Christ, reconciling the world to God's Self.

People: God no longer holds our misdeeds against us.

Pastor: Friends, believe the good news!

People: In Jesus Christ, we are forgiven.

[AND]

Exhortation

As we work together with Christ, we urge you also not to accept the grace of God in vain.

PRAYER OF THE DAY

Caring Creator and Leader, reassure us that the powers of nature are not beyond your control, nor the inner storms of our own nature beyond your quieting touch, so that we may trust you more fully and find the calm we need when circumstances threaten to swamp us. Amen

PRAYER OF THANKSGIVING

God of storm and calm, Christ of confusion and order, Spirit of gales and stillness, we are grateful to find you near whatever the weather of social or geographic circumstance. What enormous powers surround us, some that we can harness, others that we can only witness with awe. We are grateful for the camaraderie common danger may inspire among us and for the special courage so often brought out by emergencies. We give special thanks for those who have come to our aid, not least, Christ our savior. Amen

PRAYER OF DEDICATION

Let our gifts, divine Reconciler, be a sign of our faith that you will still work through your church as a ministry of reconciliation in this troubled world. Amen

PRAYERS OF INTERCESSION AND COMMEMORATION

(May be used for Father's Day)

Holy Father, Beloved Son, Family Spirit, may all earth's families at last honor your names in word and deed, giving thanks for your generous provisions for all created things. Hear our prayers for all human fathers that they may share the attributes that you honor in your word, written and alive, the qualities of strength, and patience, and perseverance. Save them from bravado, from abuse of authority, and from dishonor. Bring joy to all living fathers today, comfort to fathers near to death, and encouragement to fathers tested to their limits.

Teach the leaders of the nations also the difference between boasting and confidence, between fear and weakness, between resolve and intractability. Save us from destruction that is excused on shaky grounds of national pride that ignores the interdependence of all the earth's people for survival and peace.

Broaden the minds of all through education and the interchange of ideas and the examination of universal values and the appreciation of the best that humanity can do when reaching for the absolutes of beauty, truth, and love that are your nature. Hear our prayers for all who need us that we may serve them as you lead us to them.

God of Abraham, Isaac, and Jacob, God of Sarah, Rebekah, and Rachel, as Jesus said, you are God not of the dead, but of the living. We rejoice that you have provided an eternal home for us with your risen and exalted Son Jesus. For our physical and spiritual fathers who are now with you, we give thanks. Grant us grace to follow them in our manner of life and to love and serve you wholeheartedly and our neighbors as ourselves. To you, Fatherly, Brotherly, Motherly God we ascribe all power, and providence, and praise, time without end. Amen

Proper 8 (June 26-July 2)

First Lesson - David laments the death of King Saul and his bosom friend, Prince Jonathan. 2 Samuel 1:1, 17-27

Psalm 130

Second Lesson - Paul promotes the sharing of the Corinthians, who have the means, with those who are poor and in need of their help. 2 Corinthians 8:7-15

Gospel - Mark recounts two incidents of healing in the ministry of Jesus. Mark 5:21-43

CALL TO WORSHIP

Leader: The grace of our Lord Jesus Christ be with you all.

People: And also with you.

Leader: Seek the face of the God of Israel and of Jesus to receive the blessing of God our savior.

People: We see the face of the God our savior in the face of Jesus Christ.

INVOCATION

Loving God, we seek your face in times of joy and sorrow. We may come more casually when life is full of happiness. We come with yearning when sorrow and tragedy have shadowed our joy. Receive us in the best of times and the worst of times; through Jesus Christ our Lord. Amen

PRAYER OF CONFESSION

God of death and life, of tragedy and comedy, of sorrow and joy, we confess our dismay at the grief and accidents that you permit to happen in this world. We question the accident happening to the person whose intentions seem to be good and the good fortune that seems to attend those intent on mischief. We cannot understand why some are healed miraculously and others are allowed to suffer almost endlessly. Forgive us if we permit our doubts to threaten our commitment to you through Jesus Christ. Amen

Declaration of Pardon

Pastor: Friends, hear the good news! How generous our Lord Jesus Christ has been: he was rich, yet for our sake he became poor,

People: so that we, through his poverty, might become rich.

Pastor: Friends, believe the good news!

People: In Jesus Christ, we are forgiven.

[AND]

Exhortation

Be rich in faith, speech, knowledge, and zeal of every kind. Show yourselves lavish in generous service.

PRAYER OF THE DAY

Approachable God, may we touch you in faith and receive the cure of our spiritual and physical maladies so that we may live at peace and in freedom from what troubles us, through Jesus Christ our Savior. Amen

PRAYER OF THANKSGIVING

God of mystery, many of the things that you do are quite beyond any explanation. Other events move us to joy and dancing with music and many instruments. Let our music also express our questions, as well as our affirmations, that we may rejoice in all things, whether in a minor or a major key. Give us joy also in our work both begun and finished with satisfaction. We offer our work and our charities as thanksgiving to you, in Jesus Christ. Amen

PRAYER OF DEDICATION

You accept, O God, what we have to give and do not expect us to give what we do not have or cannot do. From what we possess and from the talents that we have, may we give without stint. Amen

PRAYERS OF INTERCESSION
AND COMMEMORATION

God of families, large and small, protoparent for all parents, hear our prayer for the whole human family. Bless those who have celebrated long marriages and extended families with connections near and far. Comfort the children and grandchildren of broken marriages as well as the partners who have known the pain and grief of separation and divorce. Encourage all who undertake the counseling of couples and families in times of crisis and distress. Prevent all of us who are married from taking for granted our spouses and families that we may seek every means to enrich and secure our marital and family ties.

Recruit for places of leadership in the nations persons with skills in communicating clearly and without equivocation that peace may not be jeopardized by bellicose threats and provocative acts, nor by protestations of peaceful intentions that are meant to obscure devious and covert belligerent activities.

Bless the leaders of our nation—executives, legislators, judges—that we may be governed conscientiously.

Be with any of our number who look to us for our prayers in time of illness and difficulty of any kind. Hear us as we name them in our hearts.

Eternal God, we remember with thanksgiving those who have loved and served you in your church on earth, who now rest from their labors, especially those most dear to us, whom we name in our hearts before you. Keep us in communion with all your saints, and bring us at last to the joy of your heavenly kingdom. Amen

Proper 9 (July 3-9)

First Lesson - David becomes king of all the tribes of Israel at Hebron. 2 Samuel 5:1-5, 9-10

Psalm 48

Second Lesson - The apostle Paul shares with some reticence a mystical experience of Paradise. 2 Corinthians 12:2-10

Gospel - Jesus faces hometown skepticism and opposition, proceding to share his spiritual power with disciples. Mark 6:1-13

CALL TO WORSHIP

Leader: The grace of our Lord Jesus Christ be with you all.

People: And also with you.

Leader: Come to worship with an honest acknowledgment of your weaknesses,

People: and the power of Christ will come and rest upon us.

145

INVOCATION

Almighty God, powerful Christ, empowering Spirit, we come to worship in all humility and weakness to be empowered in proper measure by the grace you give to the unassuming. Receive us who come in the name of Jesus Christ, your Son, our Lord. Amen

PRAYER OF CONFESSION

Sovereign of sovereigns, our ambitions do not always coincide with your priorities. We may be concerned too much about the beauty of our place of worship and concerned too little about the beauty of our lives and relationships with others. We need the mark of your grace upon us, your people, as well as a visible sanctuary for your worship. Forgive us if we are more jealous of the dignity of our name rather than yours. We pray in the name of Jesus. Amen

Declaration of Pardon

Pastor: Friends, hear the good news! God's grace is all you need.

People: Divine power comes to full strength in our weakness.

Pastor: Friends, believe the good news!

People: In Jesus Christ, we are forgiven.

[AND]

Exhortation

Prefer to find your joy and pride in the very things that are your weakness and then the power of Christ will come and rest upon you.

PRAYER OF THE DAY

Penetrating Spirit, open our minds to the wisdom we may receive from hometown prophets. Touch our hearts with healing gifts that you have granted to our neighbors, so that your work may not be obstructed by our unbelief. Amen

PRAYER OF THANKSGIVING

God of surprises, you bring the wise to birth in unlikely places and skills of art and healing from families of unpromising histories. We are grateful for all wisdom expressed in speech, in writing, in music, in arts of all kinds. We appreciate healing words and touches that make us whole, especially the words of your Son, Jesus, and the comfort of your Holy Spirit. Amen

PRAYER OF DEDICATION

O God, bind together our gifts and ourselves by the Spirit in the church, that what otherwise would be weak may be strong and what otherwise would be insufficient may be sufficient to accomplish the mission of Christ in this place and in the whole world. Amen

PRAYERS OF INTERCESSION AND COMMEMORATION

Sovereign God, peerless Christ, unsurpassed Spirit, liberate the peoples who live in countries with totalitarian regimes that seek to enforce obedience that is due only to you. Free those who are imprisoned for living and speaking the truth. Free us from addictions that destroy the body and cloud our judgment. Aid those who seek to hamper the traffic in illegal drugs, which endanger both the life of the user and society at large.

Save us from greed that consumes more than our share of the earth's resources, leaving on the deprived marks of weakness in body and limited intelligence. Give wisdom, patience, and perseverance to all who would aid in the healing of diseased and broken bodies and the recovery of mental health.

Promote among us a helping spirit that we may share the good news of Christ in word and deed, that others may trust in Christ, be joined in one Spirit, and covenant to serve you always.

We give you thanks, O God, for all who have fought the good fight and finished their race and kept the faith, and for those dear to us who are at rest with you. Grant us grace to follow them as they followed Christ. Bring us, with them, to those things that no eye has seen, nor ear heard, which you have prepared for those who love you. To your name, with the church on earth and the church in heaven, we ascribe all honor and glory, forever and ever. Amen

Proper 10 (July 10-16)

First Lesson - David's dance before the Lord is quite different from the dance before King Herod in today's Gospel. 2 Samuel 6:1-5, 12*b*-19

Psalm 24

Second Lesson - Paul rejoices in the eternal purposes of God revealed in Jesus Christ. Ephesians 1:3-14

Gospel - The martyrdom of John the Baptist is remembered long after his death and burial. Mark 6:14-29

CALL TO WORSHIP

Leader: The grace of our Lord Jesus Christ be with you all.

People: And also with you.

Leader: Believer/Priests, you are clothed with the garments of salvation.

People: As loyal servants of the heavenly realm we shout for joy.

INVOCATION

Benevolent God, you receive the worship of your varied peoples with a variety of styles of music and ritual. May our worship offer you the best we can present to you, whatever our talent, in the Spirit of Jesus Christ. Amen

PRAYER OF CONFESSION

How dangerous is the pride in which we attempt to compare our greatness to yours, O God! What lineage, however honorable, can be traced with confidence in your eternity? What national history or personal history deserves to be mentioned in connection with the history of your saving acts? Forgive the haughtiness that accompanies our pride of race, or place, or person. Only by your grace are we received into the heavenly realms, through Jesus Christ our Savior. Amen

Declaration of Pardon

Pastor: Friends, hear the good news! In Christ your release is secured

People: and our sins are forgiven through the shedding of his blood.

Pastor: Friends, believe the good news!

People: In Jesus Christ, we are forgiven.

[AND]

Exhortation

Live for the praise of God's glory.

PRAYER OF THE DAY

Lord of all being, we would offer all our artistic gifts to you rather than to any human authority, giving praise to you for all the beauty of creation by our own creativity, however modest in comparison to yours; through Jesus Christ our Redeemer. Amen

PRAYER OF THANKSGIVING

Parenting God, Adopter of children, Unifying Spirit, how can we evaluate the richness of your grace lavished on us in Jesus Christ? How can we estimate the treasure of wisdom and insight that you have graciously given us, disclosing the long-hidden purposes of your intention to unify all things in the universe in our Lord Jesus Christ? We can only praise you to the limits of our vocabulary. We can adore you to the full capacity of our loving. We can dedicate our lives to you in daily obedience to your direction. All glory be given to you, O God. Amen

PRAYER OF DEDICATION

Purposeful God, you honor us by including us in your plans for the universe. Receive our offerings and our promised willingness to fit into the place you have for us in the completion of your grand design in Jesus Christ. Amen

PRAYERS OF INTERCESSION
AND COMMEMORATION

Almighty God, in Jesus Christ, you taught us to pray, and promised that what we ask in his name will be given us. Guide us by your Holy Spirit, that our prayers may serve your will and show your steadfast love; through the same Jesus Christ our Lord.

Creator God, you made all things in your wisdom, and in your love you save us. We pray for the whole creation. Order unruly powers, deal with injustice, feed and satisfy those who thirst for justice, so that your children may freely enjoy the earth you have made, and cheerfully sing your praises; through Jesus Christ our Lord.

God of compassion, in Jesus Christ you cared for those who were blind or deaf, crippled or slow to learn. Though all of us need help, give special care to those who have handicaps, particularly those we name in silence. By our concern may they know the love you have for them and come to trust you; through Jesus Christ our healer. Amen

Eternal God, your servant, Jesus, had no place to lay his head, and no home to call his own. We pray for men and women, girls and boys, who follow seasons and go where the work is, who harvest crops or work part-time jobs. Be with them in love, so they may believe in you and be your pilgrim people, trusting in Jesus Christ the Lord.

God of compassion, we remember those who suffer want and anxiety because they have no work. Guide the people of this land to use its wealth so that all may find fulfilling employment and receive just payment for their labor, through Jesus Christ our Lord.

Comfort and relieve, O Lord, all who are in trouble, sorrow, grief, or any other need, especially those known to us, whom we name before you in silence. Heal them in body, mind, or spirit, working in them and for them gracious wonders beyond all their hopes and dreams, through Jesus Christ our Savior.

Eternal God, fulfill our desires and petitions as may be best for us; granting us in this world knowledge of your truth, and in the age to come life everlasting. God of the living, we praise you for all your servants who, having been faithful to you on earth, now live with you in heaven. Keep us in communion with them until we meet with all your children in the joy of the kingdom, through Jesus Christ our Lord. Amen

Proper 11 (July 17-23)

First Lesson - King David and the prophet Nathan discuss the building of a temple to replace the tabernacle. 2 Samuel 7:1-14*a*

Psalm 89:20-37

Second Lesson - Paul describes the new covenant that includes the Gentiles in the people of God. Ephesians 2:11-22

Gospel - Jesus and the disciples needed respite from the heavy demands of the people who looked to them for help. Mark 6:30-34

CALL TO WORSHIP

Leader: The grace of our Lord Jesus Christ be with you all.

People: And also with you.

Leader: Relax. You have heard the invitation of the Christ.

People: We have to come to this quiet place for rest and renewal.

INVOCATION

We are not like sheep without a shepherd, O God, for you have gathered us into a single people in Christ. Though we were once far off, we have been brought near by the blood of Christ, who is our peace. Receive our worship with the communion of saints through Christ Jesus our Lord. Amen

PRAYER OF CONFESSION

Divine Shepherd, you seek to gather your scattered flock and bring them back to the way of righteousness. We are sorry for whatever we have done or failed to do that has estranged others from you rather than entreating them to come back to your fold. Forgive our own wandering and ungodly actions, through Jesus Christ, who laid down his life as our Good Shepherd. Amen

Declaration of Pardon

Pastor: Friends, hear the good news! Christ proclaims peace to you who were far off.

People: **Now we are made near by the blood of his cross.**

Pastor: Friends, believe the good news!

People: **In Jesus Christ, we are forgiven.**

[AND]

Exhortation

Share the concern of Christ for his flock, that none may be without a shepherd.

PRAYER OF THE DAY

Prince and Preacher of Peace, guide us in your ways and so inspire our words and actions by your Spirit that we may make gates where there are still walls between nations and nationalities, between churches and religions, all brought nearer to our eternal Parent. Amen

PRAYER OF THANKSGIVING

From what diversity of humanity you build your church, Divine Builder! With what grace you inhabit this temple, making it holy by your presence within this human dwelling! We celebrate our foundation on apostles and prophets and especially the keystone, Jesus Christ! His cross mounted on the highest steeple cannot do justice to the miracle of reconciliation accomplished by your covenant mercies. We exalt your name, One God, Architect, Builder, Inhabiting Spirit. Amen

PRAYER OF DEDICATION

You fulfill all our needs, O God, except our need to give to others and to you. Receive our offerings for the sake of your self-giving Son, Jesus Christ. Amen

PRAYERS OF INTERCESSION AND COMMEMORATION

Creator, Redeemer, Sustainer, continue your work of creating, redeeming, and sustaining. Create new associations of people in neighborhoods and nations and internationally to accomplish your work in the world. Redeem those whose lives at present are lived for unworthy ends, but whose energies could be channeled into lines of positive accomplishment not only for themselves but for others.

Sustain those who grow weary in doing good and who see little or nothing being achieved in their efforts to serve you.

Rebuke forces of evil in the world by your continued prodding of the individual conscience and the resistance of your people to injustice and sin of every kind. With the call to repentance, send the church the good news of Christ, who continues to teach those who will be taught and heals the sick in body and mind and spirit.

Hear our prayers for the administration, legislature, and judiciary at every level of government, from village and city and county, to state and nation, that mistakes may be corrected, and honest effort made to serve all the needs of every constituency. Enable us to establish new means of distributing the good things of the earth so that nothing is wasted and no one is in want.

Shape and reshape your church to serve the needs of the present day and to be ready for the days ahead.

Eternal God, we remember before you those who have lived with us who have directed our steps in the Way, opened our eyes to the truth, inspired our hearts by their witness, and strengthen our wills by their devotion. We rejoice in their lives dedicated to your service. We honor them in their death, and pray that we may be united with them in the glory of Christ's resurrection. Amen

Proper 12 (July 24-30)

First Lesson - King David arranges the death of the husband in the attempt to cover up his adulterous affair with the wife, Bathsheba. 2 Samuel 11:1-15

Psalm 14

Second Lesson - Paul concludes a prayer for his readers with a gloria. Ephesians 3:14-21

Gospel - A miraculous feeding of a multitude and Jesus' walk on water amaze those who are there. John 6:1-21

CALL TO WORSHIP

Leader: The grace of our Lord Jesus Christ be with you all.

People: And also with you.

Leader: Come without concealment to confess your sins.

People: We will return to our homes happy that our sins have been put away!

INVOCATION

We bow before you, O God, for you are the parent from whom every family in heaven and on earth takes its name. We pray that, according to the riches of your glory, you will grant that we may be strengthened in our inner being with power through the Spirit, that Christ may dwell in our hearts through faith. In his name. Amen

PRAYER OF CONFESSION

God of nations, Sovereign of sovereigns, Protector of people, we do not understand why the innocent suffer for the sins of the guilty and the weak for the faults of the strong. We are strong in our denunciation of the sins of others and loud in our demands for their punishment. We are apologetic in the admission of our own sins and plaintive in our cries for mercy. Forgive our double standard, and grant us pardon for our offenses through Jesus our advocate. Amen

Declaration of Pardon

Pastor: Friends, hear the good news! God has laid on the crucified Christ the consequences of our sins,

People: so that we will not die.

Pastor: Friends, believe the good news!

People: In Jesus Christ, we are forgiven.

[AND]

Exhortation

Grasp what is the breadth and length and height and depth of the love of Christ, and to know it, though it is beyond knowledge. So may you attain to fullness of being, the fullness of God.

PRAYER OF THE DAY

Modest Master, teach us to withdraw from the praise that would put us in the power of others and prevent our doing what you want us to do and when. Amen

PRAYER OF THANKSGIVING

God of all families in heaven and earth, receive our praise and thanksgiving for the manifestation of your love for us all in Jesus Christ. You do for us immeasurably more than we can ask or think. Your Spirit enriches our lives with a sense of your presence within us, as well as around us, and empowers our common service in the church of your dear Son. In generation after generation you inspire faith in Christ and regenerate your people. For all that you do, we give thanks. For all that you are, we give praise, endlessly. Amen

PRAYER OF DEDICATION

Generous God, show us again what miracles you can do when we offer to you all that we have and all that we are, no matter how insignificant it may seem, through Jesus Christ our Lord. Amen

PRAYERS OF INTERCESSION AND COMMEMORATION

Limitless God, Self-limited Christ, Unlimited Spirit, your love seeks to redeem all who will respond to your invitation and to incorporate them into the body of Christ, your visible agency for the accomplishment of your loving purposes in the world. Enliven your people that they may not be weary in doing good but faithful always in answer to your call to duty and beyond duty to daring. Give courage to attempt what has not been done before but which seems the inspired thing to do, not for the glory of the doer but for the glory of God. Sovereign of sovereigns, let your authority to call to account be remembered by all who take lightly the responsibility of high office, and use their position for less than just designs. Creator of all good things, inspire the creative among us to find new ways of employing the talents of human workers, that the unemployed may be put to work at what is more than busyness, making our communities more beautiful, more healthful, more friendly in every way. Redeemer of the lost and the wasted, motivate the drifter and the purposeless in a search for their place in your design for humanity that they may find meaning in their existence and real direction for living. Divine Healer, lead medical researchers in their search for cures to our ailments and enable all medical practitioners to use the best available remedies to heal our infirmities. Hear our prayers for all who need your healing and help, whom we name in our hearts before you.

Eternal God, we remember before you those who have lived with us who have directed our steps in the Way, opened our eyes to the truth, inspired our hearts by their witness, and strengthen our wills by their devotion. We rejoice in their lives dedicated to your service. We honor them in their death, and pray that we may be united with them in the glory of Christ's resurrection. Amen

Proper 13 (July 31-August 6)

First Lesson - The prophet's parable traps King David's conscience. 2 Samuel 11:26–12:13*a*

Psalm 51:1-12

Second Lesson - The unity of the church can be maintained only by the exercise of the best gifts that God gives. Ephesians 4:1-6

Gospel - Jesus advocates a higher vocation than the pursuit of a free lunch. John 6:24-35

CALL TO WORSHIP

Leader: The grace of our Lord Jesus Christ be with you all.

People: And also with you.

Leader: Come into God's presence with a clean heart, with a new and right spirit.

People: We will worship in the discipline of the Holy Spirit.

INVOCATION

Holy God, Parent of all, in Jesus Christ you have called us to lead a life like his, with all humility and gentleness, with patience, bearing with one another in love, making every effort to maintain the unity of the Spirit in the bond of peace. We come to worship you in this Spirit in his name. Amen

PRAYER OF CONFESSION

Giver of manna, Breaker of bread, Creator of the new, it is true that we still do what we have not learned from Christ. We can be hard-hearted when we should be forgiving. We can be selfish when we should be willing to share. We can be greedy and complaining when we have enough to get by. We can be as unscrupulous in our dealing as if we did not know what is just and true. Forgive us and finish your new creation through Jesus Christ. Amen

Declaration of Pardon

Pastor: Friends, hear the good news! Hope is held out in God's call to you.

People: One Christ, one faith, one baptism, one God, parent of us all.

Pastor: Friends, believe the good news!

People: In Jesus Christ, we are forgiven.

[AND]

Exhortation

Be humble always, and gentle, and patient too. Be forbearing with one another and charitable.

PRAYER OF THE DAY

Giver of good things, Gift of God, Spirit of the self-giver, give us an appetite for the eternal life that we may not be satisfied with what perishes, but devote our lives to the pursuit of spiritual excellence. Amen

PRAYER OF THANKSGIVING

Giver of all patience, Child of our humanity, renewing Spirit, we turn from our complaints about what we do not have to thanksgiving for the many good things you have given us. In addition to the simple nutrition of good bread and butter, you give us the bread of angels, sustenance of the Spirit, the bread of life. We rejoice in the ideas and revelation that stimulate our thinking. We revel in the new joys that we experience in the shared intimacy of others with similar commitments to the truth. We are grateful for your patience in teaching us, your understanding through incarnational experience, your perseverance in developing our relationships. All praise to you perfect Parent, loving Brother, family Spirit. Amen

PRAYER OF DEDICATION

Generous Giver, we would emulate your generosity, making possible the sharing of bread of life at the Lord's table, and in the gathering of your people where they live and work and play, everywhere. Amen

PRAYERS OF INTERCESSION AND COMMEMORATION

Our Patron, Our Sponsor, Our Matron, with what solicitude you care for your people. Continue to show your provision for the whole human family by inspiring generosity in those of us who have to share with those who do not. Save us from selfishness that insists in holding on to what we could really spare for the benefit of the truly impoverished. Give us courage to be advocates for those who cannot speak for themselves, those who have no power to strike for higher wages because they do not have work, those who live far from the centers of wealth and without the means to make their needs known without the voice of the church and other agencies of relief.

Encourage governments and both labor and management in our nation and other countries to find ways of sharing ideas and work that will be to the advantage of all who need work and its rewards. Bless agencies of mutual help that bring encouragement to the troubled, whether they be troubled by alcoholism or other addiction, or emotional distress, or single parenting. Break down the pride that prevents some who need such help to seek it for themselves and then in turn share their experience by helping others.

Great Physician, heal those whose illness is beyond the skill of human medicine, as well as those in the care of our hospitals and clinics and nursing services. Grant wisdom to all who are in a position to improve and expand the availability of such services.

God of all times and places, we praise you for all your servants who, having been faithful to you on earth, now live with you in heaven. Keep us in communion with them until we meet with all your children in the joy of your eternal kingdom; through Jesus Christ our Lord. Amen

Proper 14 (August 7-13)

First Lesson - King David mourns the murder of his rebellious son, Absalom. 2 Samuel 18:5 9, 15, 31-33

Psalm 130

Second Lesson - The apostle Paul mentions some daily specifics of morality that should reflect Christian faith. Ephesians 4:25–5:2

Gospel - The messianic claim of Jesus is expressed in the metaphor of heavenly manna. John 6:35, 41-51

CALL TO WORSHIP

Leader: The grace of our Lord Jesus Christ be with you all.

People: And also with you.

Leader: Await God's presence and hope in God's word.

People: We will attend as if we were looking for the first light of dawn after a dark night.

INVOCATION

As your Perfect Son, Jesus, went habitually to the synagogue, God of Israel and the church, so we come to this house of prayer in imitation of his faithfulness. Grant that we may see more light dawning on our minds and hearts as we hear your word and offer obedient service to you and your people; through Jesus Christ our Lord. Amen

PRAYER OF CONFESSION

Loving and forgiving Parent, Loving and forgiving Christ, Loving and forgiving Spirit, we confess that we are not always generous, tenderhearted and forgiving. We can be spiteful in our behavior because of the bad feeling that we cherish in our hearts. That anger can come out in angry shouting and cursing, which is not only offensive to others but grieves your Spirit within us. Forgive us for resisting the Spirit who is at work in us to make us more like Jesus Christ. Amen

Declaration of Pardon

Pastor: Friends, hear the good news! God in Christ has forgiven you.

People: Christ gave himself on our behalf as an offering and sacrifice whose fragrance is pleasing to God.

Pastor: Friends, believe the good news!
People: In Jesus Christ, we are forgiven.

[AND]

Exhortation

Be generous to one another, tenderhearted, forgiving one another as God in Christ forgave you.

PRAYER OF THE DAY

Foster son of Joseph, very Son of God, so teach us your way of self-giving that we may give ourselves in the service of others as you have given yourself for the life of the world. Amen

PRAYER OF THANKSGIVING

God of meadow and wilderness, Christ of human experience, Spirit of renewal and rest, we are thankful for the angel you send to minister to us. When we are depressed and ready to die, you send someone with a word of encouragement, or a gift of food or flowers, or an invitation that leads to a change of scene and an opportunity to recover and go on. When our chins are on our chests, you send someone with a loving touch to raise our eyes to you. Joy and thanksgiving break through the clouds like the sun after a storm. We exalt your name together, ever-loving Parent, understanding Brother, Holy Spirit of God, eternal and liberating. Amen

PRAYER OF DEDICATION

As God's dear children, we come to you, trying to be like Jesus Christ, who loved you and gave himself up on our behalf as an offering and sacrifice whose fragrance is pleasing to you. Receive what we give of ourselves and of our name in the name of Jesus Christ. Amen

PRAYER OF INTERCESSION
AND COMMEMORATION

God of old, God of young, God unaging, hear the prayers of your people at all stages of their lives. When we are older we are uncertain with the onset of physical problems that are new to us, which make us more apprehensive as to the length of our days. When we are young we are impatient to have what others have and to do what we have been unable so far to do. In middle years we are confused and often wonder whether we have done anything worthwhile or ought to try something other than what we have been doing. Be our guide "while life shall last and our eternal home."

God of all nations, direct the leaders of nations large and small in the search for justice and peace. Remind those impatient to gain their political ends by violent means that there is little to be gained by provocation rather than persuasion.

Guide all educators who look for innovative ways to stimulate the desire to learn among those who find learning difficult or boring. Give insight and patience to all who teach in church and school.

Move the creative to find new modes of communication that will increase social awareness of common achievements and as yet unreached goals.

Save us from those so greedy as to exploit the grievous needs of the hungry of the world for their own wealth. Give to those working under difficult circumstances the endless patience and perseverance to serve the suffering in what appear to be hopeless circumstances.

Hear our prayers for those who suffer from unidentified illness, and from illnesses that, though diagnosed, are beyond our present knowledge to cure. Give assurance to all whose days are numbered that you have not forgotten them and have a place prepared for all who love you and the family of God.

God of all times and places, we praise you for all your servants who having been faithful to you on earth, now live with you in heaven. Keep us in communion with them until we meet with all your children in the joy of your eternal kingdom; through Jesus Christ our Lord. Amen

Proper 15 (August 14-20)

First Lesson - Solomon comes to the throne after the death of King David. 1 Kings 2:10-12; 3:3-14

Psalm 111

Second Lesson - Paul admonishes the Ephesians to live carefully but joyfully. Ephesians 5:15-20

Gospel - To the imagery of the living bread, Jesus adds the symbol of the cup. John 6:51-58

CALL TO WORSHIP

Leader: The grace of our Lord Jesus Christ be with you all.

People: And also with you.

Leader: Praise the Lord! Give thanks to the Lord!

People: We will give thanks to the Lord with all our heart.

INVOCATION

To you, God our Parent, we give thanks at all times and for everything. Now we come in the Spirit, to sing psalms and hymns and spiritual songs, making melody with heart and voice in the name of our Lord Jesus Christ. Amen

PRAYER OF CONFESSION

Wise God, forgive our foolish preoccupation with things that don't matter. We are reluctant to open our minds to new ideas and broader views. We are content to love you with less than all our minds. We resist the discipline of study and sharing and self-evaluation that could help us to grow in wisdom like your Son, Jesus Christ. Amen

Declaration of Pardon

Pastor: Friends, hear the good news! Jesus said, "As the living Father sent me, and I live because of the Father, so he who eats in remembrance of me shall live because of me."

People: We shall live because we eat his bread and drink his cup.

Pastor: Friends, believe the good news!

People: In Jesus Christ, we are forgiven.

[AND]

Exhortation

Be most careful how you conduct yourselves: like sensible people, not thoughtlessly. Use the present opportunity to the full, for these are evil days.

PRAYER OF THE DAY

Whet our appetite, Giver of life, for the bread of life, Jesus Christ, that through our faith in him and our reception of him we may have life eternal, living with him day by day and raised by him on the last day. Amen

PRAYER OF THANKSGIVING

Founder of the feast, we give thanks today and every day for daily bread to sustain our bodies and the bread of life to restore our souls. We speak to one another in psalms and sing songs and hymns in praise of your goodness in the name or our Lord Jesus Christ. In silent times we make music in our hearts, full of joy, full of the Holy Spirit. For all who write words that we can say or sing, we express our gratitude. For all who compose melodies that give zest to our celebration of your grace, we speak our praise. All praise to you, God of wisdom, beauty, and truth. Amen

PRAYER OF DEDICATION

Creator and giver of all good things, we bring our offering of thanksgiving and declare our intentions to turn from evil and do good, to seek peace and pursue it. Teach us how to revere your name more fully through Jesus Christ our Lord. Amen

PRAYERS OF INTERCESSION
AND COMMEMORATION

God of clouds and fire, Christ of passion and peace, Spirit of conflict and resolution, reveal yourself to us in all the circumstances of our lives. Do you play hide and seek with us to distract us from the pursuits of the trivial? Is your mystery intentional or just the taxing of our limited minds or short attention spans? On the human scene, teach us to listen behind the form of words to the sounds of emotion, to discern the echo of hollowness, to detect the haughtiness of arrogance, to measure the strength of challenge, to plumb the depths of sincerity, to discover hidden agendas, to gauge the degree of honesty. Teach us to be straightforward in our own speaking that we may not hide from each other in endless games of confusion and misunderstanding.

As we are organized in various organizations and governments, help us find means of change that are less costly in human suffering, in the death of the innocent as well as the involved, the maiming of the onlookers and the unprotected. Teach us to define our quality of life in more than profits and losses showing appreciation of the need to take care of the earth and its water and air for the health of all living things.

Grant to your church increasing effectiveness in manifesting your love in both the personal attitudes of each of us and also in the social expression of our common faith. Widen our understanding and open us up where we have been closed to new insights and greater love. Show us new ways of transcending economic problems that will not deprive some to enrich others and create divisions between people and nations. Help us to do what we can to solve problems of unemployment and poverty in our own neighborhoods, as well as support the mission of the church and international relief agencies.

Hear our prayers for those persons who are looking to us today for our intercessions. Minister to them as you know they have need.

Eternal God, we remember before you those who have lived with us who have directed our steps in the Way, opened our eyes to the truth, inspired our hearts by their witness, and strengthen our wills by their devotion. We rejoice in their lives dedicated to your service. We honor them in their death, and pray that we may be united with them in the glory of Christ's resurrection. Amen

Proper 16 (August 21-27)

First Lesson - Solomon prays solemnly when the ark of the covenant is brought into the inner sanctuary of the newly built temple. 1 Kings 8:(1, 6, 10-11), 22-30, 41-43

Psalm 84

Second Lesson - The apostle Paul compares our spiritual struggles to a soldier's duty. Ephesians 6:10-20

Gospel - The sacramental significance of the death of Jesus Christ is taught by him and recorded by John. John 6:56-69

CALL TO WORSHIP

Leader: The grace of our Lord Jesus Christ be with you all.

People: And also with you.

Leader: Come to Christ whose words are words of eternal life.

People: We have faith knowing that Jesus is the Holy One of God.

INVOCATION

In this house of prayer, O God, we invoke your name. There is no one like you who keeps covenant and steadfast love for your servants who walk before you with all their heart. Not only have you lived on earth in Christ, but by the Spirit live in our hearts. Regard our prayers in the name of Jesus. Amen

PRAYER OF CONFESSION

God of the promise, you have declared yourself to be our heavenly Parent through Jesus Christ. Forgive our denial of your promised care through anxiety and our hesitancy to identify ourselves with you despite your past provision for our needs. We are sorry for the disloyalty we have shown you from time to time through our rejection of the church. Absolve us for the sake of your ever loyal Son, Jesus Christ. Amen

Declaration of Pardon

Pastor: Friends, hear the good news! Christ loved the church and gave himself for it, to consecrate it, cleansing it by water and word

People: **so that he might present the church to himself all glorious, with no stain or wrinkle or anything of the sort, but holy and without blemish.**

Pastor: Friends, believe the good news!

People: **In Jesus Christ, we are forgiven.**

[AND]

Exhortation

As members of the church, be subject to Christ, and husbands and wives be subject to each other out of reverence for Christ.

PRAYER OF THE DAY

Faithful God, when others leave you and your word, help us to be true to your Son, Jesus, no matter how hard that choice is and how unpopular. Steady us in our resolve to serve you always and to seek no easier service through Jesus Christ our Lord. Amen

PRAYER OF THANKSGIVING

Loving God, we sing your praise and shout for joy at the thought of your unstinting generosity and unflagging help. You sustain us in physical, mental, and spiritual life. You provide support for us in the life of the church and the intimacy of marriage. You are gracious and good and we honor you, God of Israel, Ruler of the church, universal Spirit. Amen

PRAYER OF DEDICATION

Christ our Lord, Head of the church, receive what we offer as members of your body. As we serve you, coordinate our efforts so that nothing that should be done is left undone and all your purposes accomplished to the glory of your name. Amen

PRAYERS OF INTERCESSION
AND COMMEMORATION

God our Creator, God our Savior, God our Sustainer, we know you are beyond our reach and control and that we cannot contain your presence in the most magnificent temples, cathedrals, or mosques. Yet these places are hallowed by our prayers. May our reverence for the house of prayer be an example to our neighbors. Spare us the desecration of those who proclaim their narrow politics with graffiti and hateful signs and symbols. Help all people of prayer to carry their faith with them into the political scene, frankly sharing their beliefs without seeking to impose them on others by verbal threats or actual violence. Let us find the common ground on which we can meet with mutual respect and tolerance that can proceed to loving our neighbors as ourselves.

Though we seek a measure of serenity, keep us from cowardice in the face of what can be changed. Help us first to model the values that we honor so that our speech is not seen as hypocritical and contrary to our actual way of life. May we seek consensus with others as to what is best for all of us, learning to speak the truth as we see it with love and not arrogance.

May our own peace of mind and trust in your providence be an example for those who are confused, depressed, or anxious. Great Physician, heal our illnesses and disease of body, mind, and spirit. No earthly sanctuary, even the most magnificent, can match the eternal sanctuary that your Son is preparing for us in order to be close to and with you, Eternal Parent. We rejoice in the security of those you have already taken to yourself and pray that your mothering spirit will lead us gently but surely on the way that leads to eternal life. We will praise you here and hereafter. Amen

Proper 17 (August 28-September 3)

First Lesson - A romantic song of love includes a touch of spring fever. Song of Solomon 2:8-13

Psalm 45:1-2, 6-9. A love song.

[OR]

Psalm 45:1-2, 6-9

Second Lesson - This reading introduces the "wisdom literature" of the New Testament. James 1:17-27

Gospel - Jesus teaches that genuine purity is in our inner life, not merely ceremonial sanctity. Mark 7:1-8, 14-15, 21-23

CALL TO WORSHIP

Leader: The grace of our Lord Jesus Christ be with you all.

People: And also with you.

Leader: Give yourselves wholly to prayer ... always interceding for all God's people, and pray for me that I may be granted the right words to make known God's purpose.

People: We will give ourselves wholly to prayer, always interceding for all God's people, and pray for you that you may be granted the right words to make known God's purpose.

INVOCATION

Father of lights, with whom there is no variation or shadow due to change, we worship you as those who are reborn by the word of truth. We present ourselves as a kind of firstfruits of Jesus Christ. Receive us for his sake. Amen

PRAYER OF CONFESSION

God above us, God around us, God within us, help us to distinguish between your law and the traditions of our society. We are prone to make decisions on opinions that "everyone is doing it" or that polls show us that we have a lot of company. Forgive our neglect of the inner life when you have told us that it is from within us, and not from outside us, that comes a horrendous catalogue of sins. Save us from all our sins, divine Redeemer. Amen

Declaration of Pardon

Pastor: Friends, hear the good news! The Spirit will give us inner strength to resist all evil.

People: And our heavenly Parent gives the Holy Spirit at our request.

Pastor: Friends, believe the good news!

People: In Jesus Christ, we are forgiven.

[AND]

Exhortation

Find your strength in the power of the Spirit so that you may be able to stand firm against all the devices of the devil.

PRAYER OF THE DAY

Sovereign Spirit, so order our thoughts that our actions may give evidence of your inner rule in our lives and our worship be no vain lip service, but heartfelt obedience to your commands. Amen

PRAYER OF THANKSGIVING

God our guardian, we give hearty thanks that you do not leave us defenseless against the evil around us or already within us. Not only our physical safety but our spiritual security are of concern to you. We appreciate the many resources you have given us to fight against the ploys of the evil one. We enjoy the community of faith that supports us in our striving against sin. We rejoice in the victory of Christ over sin and death and will celebrate that conquest in eternity. Amen

PRAYER OF DEDICATION

Divine Commander, with all your people we would stand firm in support of your cause and in opposition to the dark forces of heaven and earth. Receive this pledge and these tokens of our allegiance. Amen

PRAYERS OF INTERCESSION AND COMMEMORATION

Loving God, Compassionate Christ, Caring Spirit, we pray for lovers young and old and middle-aged that they may find their feelings returned in the same measure as they give their love. Beyond romantic feelings give fidelity to them and their mates that they may share good times and bad times, happy times and sad times, springtime, summertime, wintertime, year after year.

Grant wisdom to those who counsel those to be married and grace to those working out difficulties in their relationship.

Strengthen our society in its ability to care for children in families through the loving care of both parents and in substitute families for those who are orphaned. May we not put economic prosperity and corporate profits above the adequate care of children with working parents.

Continue among us gifted writers and composers and movie makers who can express true love songs, and stories and movies that appreciate constancy and caring, mutuality and sharing.

Grant to the church loving openness to the single and to

lesbian and gay people that they may find friendship among us and not be lonely. Spare all minorities the ostracism that has been all too common in society and the workplace.

Grant your blessing to all who practice the arts of reconciliation: the domestic and social and racial and economic and political peacemakers.

Increase the numbers of philanthropists who share the fruits of their prosperity with the disadvantaged and find places of service for those of limited abilities as well as the very gifted.

May the church give leadership in not only doing good, but also in saying what is good so that the gospel is not despised as worthless. Save us from preaching what we will not practice, unlike the consistency of Jesus. Through Christ our Lord. Amen

Proper 18 (September 4-10)

First Lesson - Here is a sampling of Old Testament wisdom. Proverbs 22:1-2, 8-9, 22-23

Psalm 125

Second Lesson - The wisdom of the church, like the wisdom of Israel, is concerned for justice for the poor. James 2:1-10, (11-13), 14-17

Gospel - The healing ministry of Jesus extends beyond the borders of Israel. Mark 7:24-37

CALL TO WORSHIP

Leader: The grace of our Lord Jesus Christ be with you all.

People: **And also with you.**

Leader: Praise the Lord as long as you live.

People: **We will sing psalms to God all our life long.**

INVOCATION

God our Maker, Creator of the rich and the poor alike, may our worship be inspired by your Spirit so that what we hear and what we promise in obedience to your word in Christ may be evident in our daily life through Jesus Christ our Lord. Amen

PRAYER OF CONFESSION

Just God, you are even-handed in your justice and in the day of judgment will not play favorites. We confess that we are not so fair in our dealings. We are often unduly impressed by the powerful and the clever and excuse in them what we would condemn in the powerless and ignorant. Forgive superficiality and neglect of people needing advocacy and friendship, through the friend of sinners, Jesus Christ. Amen

Declaration of Pardon

Pastor: Friends, hear the good news! God has chosen those who are poor in the eyes of the world to be rich in faith.

People: **We will inherit the kingdom Christ has promised to those who love him.**

Pastor: Friends, believe the good news!

People: **In Jesus Christ, we are forgiven.**

[AND]

Exhortation

Never show snobbery, believing as you do in our Lord Jesus Christ who reigns in glory.

PRAYER OF THE DAY

Divine Physician, heal our hardness of hearing and soften our feelings so that we have your sensitivity to and awareness of the needs of others, often hidden behind a curtain of words. Free our tongues to share our innermost feeling with a trusted friend or counselor. Make us well, Jesus. Amen

PRAYER OF THANKSGIVING

We praise you, God of Israel, God of the church universal. You made the heavens and the earth, the sparrow and the gull, the whale and the minnow. You care for people, the hungry and the oppressed. You restore sight and help the stooped to stand tall. You give new heart to the bereaved and hopeless. Our hopes are in you and you will not disappoint us at the last. We praise you, Creator, Christ, Comforter. Amen

PRAYER OF DEDICATION

Divine Person, beyond all human personhood, transform these tangible but impersonal things into acts and gifts of persons serving persons in the name of Jesus Christ. Amen

PRAYERS OF INTERCESSION AND COMMEMORATION
(May be used for Labor Day Sunday)

God of all work, who created for six days and rested on the seventh, bless all who work to create things of beauty and things of utility from the elements that you made from nothing. Divine Redeemer, direct and teach all who repair and renew what has been broken and no longer works as it should. Bless those who care for people who cannot care for themselves.

Healing Spirit, inspire with loving wisdom those who counsel any who have lost their way and are seeking new direction and are having difficulty getting it all together.

Head of the church, so enable your body to respond with fidelity to all that you command that your work may proceed with little interruption and the goals you have set be achieved in our community and our world, which is really yours.

Governor of governors, bring a fuller measure of justice to our world, that the rights of all may be protected, from childhood to old age, from the simplest worker to the most responsible manager, male and female, all created in your image.

Free us from any activity that is a detriment to ourselves and to others. Grant us all joy in our work that we may have satisfaction in knowing that what we do makes a difference for good, benefiting our common life.

God our Creator, you have created people who go out to their work and to their labor until the evening. We rejoice both in our vocation and our retirement. The rest at the end of the day is sweeter after a day of good work. The retirement at the end of years is satisfying when we can look back at what our work has helped to accomplish.

We celebrate also the rest you have prepared for the people of God. We rejoice in the memory of those who rest from their labor, and their good works follow them to heaven by your gracious acceptance in Jesus Christ. May we not work for the food that perishes, but for the food that endures for eternal life, which the Son of Man will give. So by your earthly sacraments prepare us for the heavenly rest, through Jesus Christ, who finished his work, to whom with you and the Holy Spirit be all glory and praise, time without end. Amen

Proper 19 (September 11-17)

First Lesson - Wisdom is personified by the writer as the Word of God, and will, thereafter, be incarnate in a human person. Proverbs 1:20-33

Psalm 19

[OR]

Wisdom 7:26–8:1

Second Lesson - James describes the havoc created by uncontrolled talk and vicious cursing. James 3:1-12

Gospel - Jesus clarifies the nature of his mission as Messiah as that of a sufferer rather than a conqueror, and calls his disciples to continue to follow in similar fashion. Mark 8:27-38

CALL TO WORSHIP

Leader: The grace of our Lord Jesus Christ be with you all.

People: And also with you.

Leader: Love the Lord, who has heard us and listens to our prayers.

People: God has given us a hearing whenever we have cried out to heaven.

INVOCATION

God of glory, Son of humanity ascended to glory, Eternal Spirit, we worship you in all humility and gratitude. We are not ashamed of Jesus our Savior in his humility nor in his majesty. Receive our worship in the name of the One who loved us and gave himself for us, Jesus the Christ. Amen

PRAYER OF CONFESSION

Living and loving God, we worship you more readily in the presence of your friends than in the company of your detractors. We don't find much blessedness in being persecuted and avoid confessing our faith rather than expose ourselves to ridicule or suffering. We do not have the courage of our convictions and play safe much of the time. Forgive our failure to live our supposed faith and to act on our declared sympathies through your long-suffering Son, Jesus Christ. Amen

Declaration of Pardon

Pastor: Friends, hear the good news! Gracious is the Lord and righteous; our God is full of compassion.

People: When we are brought low, God saves us.

Pastor: Friends, believe the good news!

People: In Jesus Christ, we are forgiven.

[AND]

Exhortation

Leave self behind, take up your cross and follow Jesus. Walk in the Lord's presence in the land of the living.

PRAYER OF THE DAY

Suffering Savior, Son of the suffering God, grant us courage to accept suffering as well as healing and help for your name's sake. Give us inner strength in the Spirit to be faithful by the confession of your name, Jesus Christ, Son of the living God. Amen

PRAYER OF THANKSGIVING

God of life and health, we would thank you for health by caring for the sick. We should show our gratitude for freedom by working for the release of prisoners. We double our enjoyment of what we have by sharing with those who don't have. We echo the good news we have heard to those who live in the sadness of bad times. Receive the worship we present in word and deed in the Spirit of Jesus our Lord. Amen

PRAYER OF DEDICATION

Sovereign Lord, let our money talk for us in the hour of prayer, but also use it to send a word to the weary, to strengthen and to heal the sick in the name of Jesus. Amen

PRAYERS OF INTERCESSION AND COMMEMORATION
(May be used for Sunday prior to the beginning of the school year)

Source of wisdom, wise Teacher, Spirit of wisdom, continue to teach your church—members old and young—that the world may be instructed as well in what is true and good and beautiful. Save us from making pronouncements that issue from partial understanding and limited information.

Bless our schools with teachers and administrators who appreciate knowledge and truth in its fullness and are committed to pass along that wisdom as skillfully as they are able. Help those who write textbooks to be fair and thorough in their writing of history that our understanding of the past may be as clear and unprejudiced as is humanly possible.

Grant to parents patience in teaching their children, by word and example, manners that show respect to others and give themselves dignity worthy of regard. Teach us due regard for our bodies that we may live healthfully and teach our children to do the same. May our homes be schools for prayer that we may teach our children the great prayers of the church's past and also the attitude of humility that addresses you with love and honesty.

Bestow on leaders of governments at every level an enlarged view of what serves the common good and what is of advantage only to the few that the greatest benefit for all may be their conscious choice.

Give us wisdom in our relationships with those who are sick in body, mind, or spirit that we may do for them what is helpful, encourage them in what they can do for themselves, and commit to you what is beyond our doing. In life and in death we are yours, O God, and you are able to keep us from falling, and to make us stand without blemish in the presence of your glory with rejoicing. We give thanks for those known and dear to us who already share your glory in heaven. You are the only God, our Savior, through Jesus Christ our Lord to whom the Holy Spirit be glory, majesty, power, and authority, before all time and now and forever. Amen

Proper 20 (September 18-24)

First Lesson - The wise man describes the qualities and occupations of a capable wife. Proverbs 31:10-31

Psalm 1

Second Lesson - James advocates heavenly wisdom as opposed to selfish human behavior. James 3:13–4:3, 7-8*a*

Gospel - Jesus makes clear that worldly ambitions for prominence are less important in his domain than openness to children. Mark 9:30-37

CALL TO WORSHIP

Leader: The grace of our Lord Jesus Christ be with you all.

People: **And also with you.**

Leader: Turn your thoughts to God who is your helper.

People: **God will be the mainstay of our lives.**

INVOCATION

We draw near to you, O God, in the expectation that the Spirit will bring us into communion with you. We confess Jesus to be our champion against the powers of evil and seek his power to resist all evil in and around us. In his name. Amen

PRAYER OF CONFESSION

God of the gospel, the One who sends, the One who is sent and returns, the One who is sent and remains with the church, we declare our need of the wisdom that is from above, pure, peace-loving, considerate, open to reason. We can be devious rather than straightforward, hypocritical rather than sincere, unforgiving rather than merciful, cruel rather than kind. Forgive the bitter jealousy that leads to quarreling, the selfish ambition that destroys those who are in the way, the ungoverned passions that lead to disorder and evil of every kind. Temper your justice with mercy for the sake of your obedient Son, Jesus our peacemaker. Amen

Declaration of Pardon

Pastor: Friends, hear the good news! God comes to those who welcome even a child in the name of Jesus.

People: **We receive God when we receive Jesus and the children he loves.**

Pastor: Friends, believe the good news!

People: **In Jesus Christ, we are forgiven.**

[AND]

Exhortation

Show wisdom and understanding by deeds done in the humility that comes from wisdom.

PRAYER OF THE DAY

Galilean Jesus, mortal human, living Christ, teach us the greatness that is expressed by the embrace of a child rather than by rubbing shoulders with the powerful so that we may serve in the manner of your servanthood. Amen

PRAYER OF THANKSGIVING

God of wisdom, you are generous in sharing your wisdom with all who are receptive. Loving God, your kindness is exemplified in the humanity of Jesus and his openness to children. Spirit of peace, you can pacify our aggressiveness with our enemies. We are grateful for all that you have done for us in the events of Good Friday, and Easter, and Pentecost. We appreciate the kindly deeds you have inspired to diminish the evils that still abound in our sinful world. With thanksgiving for what you have enabled your people to reap from the seeds of peace, we look for the further harvest of peacemaking: true justice. All praise be given to you, O God. Amen

PRAYER OF DEDICATION

What we give to you, we give willingly in praise of your name for that is good. We have gathered to worship you, and we go out to serve you more humbly than before, with the help that you continue to give. Amen

PRAYERS OF INTERCESSION AND COMMEMORATION

Paternal, Fraternal, Maternal God, hear our prayers for the whole human family. Teach the world family the need for both work and play that none may be exploited by lack of proper rest and recreation along with work and study. Help business and governments to find orderly changes that provide working mothers and fathers with childcare that is safe and healthy. May we learn to share responsibility for ourselves and one another, not overworking some and leaving other idle and unemployed.

Grant wisdom and self-control to all who pilot planes, drive buses or trains, and pilot ships. Grant a change of heart to those who operate cars and trucks with reckless abandon to the harm of others and themselves.

Help us find more cooperative ways of educating our children so that none are neglected: schools and agencies and families working as teams for the nurture and love of all children. Save us from the marketers of sex that exploit the innocence of children and the naive.

Help us to find homes for the homeless and humane care for those unable to care for themselves, whatever their age or mental capacity.

Teach us the wisdom that finds beauty in what people do and how they care for others rather than superficial appearances and sensational apparel. May we respect accomplishments that serve the common welfare, that bridge barriers, that overcome prejudices, that solve problems, that diminish disease and promote healing and health.

Eternal God, we rejoice in your empire of excellence and live in the hope of ultimate perfection as you are nurturing your adopted children to be brothers and sisters of your perfect Son, Jesus Christ.

We crave the completion of our spiritual maturity beyond death and seek to follow Jesus even now as we rejoice in the provision you have made in heaven for our loved ones who have preceded us. With them we will honor and worship you in eternity, Fatherly, Brotherly, Motherly God. Amen

Proper 21 (September 25-October 1)

First Lesson - Queen Esther is a personal champion for her oppressed people. Esther 7:1-6, 9-10; 9:20-22

Psalm 124

Second Lesson - The elders are given a healing role in the life of the congregation. James 5:13-20

Gospel - Self-control is not easy but it is urgent. Mark 9:38-50

CALL TO WORSHIP

Leader: The grace of our Lord Jesus Christ be with you all.

People: And also with you.

Leader: Praise the name of the Lord, you servants of the Lord, who stand in the house of the Lord.

People: We will hallow the sacred name in this sanctuary and wherever we go.

INVOCATION

We are your servants, O God, come to receive our instructions from you as revealed in your written word and exampled in the life of Jesus, your Son. Let your Spirit empower us in our worship and in our daily service; through Jesus Christ our Lord. Amen

PRAYER OF CONFESSION

Most powerful Judge, you hear the outcry of the powerless who are defrauded by the rich. You know without our telling you that we have frequently envied the wealthy even though we know that their possessions do not withstand death and decay. Forgive us if we have conspired with any to deny the rights of the poor or withheld from anyone the simplest help we were asked to give. You will, at the last, set all things right, rewarding even the most humble service, as promised by Jesus, our Messiah. Amen

Declaration of Pardon

Pastor: Friends, hear the good news! The Lord will give his people justice and have compassion on his servants.

People: The Lord will give his people peace and joy.

Pastor: Friends, believe the good news!

People: In Jesus Christ, we are forgiven.

[AND]

Exhortation

Do not try to stop anyone who does work of divine power in the name of Jesus. Whoever is not against us is on our side.

PRAYER OF THE DAY

Jesus, Messiah, Champion of God's rule, help us to gain control of our bodies so that we restrain all harmful actions and are free to serve others in modest ways that many may not notice, but which will be rewarded by you, from whom nothing is hidden. Amen

PRAYER OF THANKSGIVING

We praise you, O God, for though you do what you please, your pleasure is justice with compassion. We worship you, O God, for though you choose your servants as you wish, your elect people are called to serve all in obedience to you. We are awed by the powers of nature, but assured that there is no force or being that can overpower you. We are most grateful that you make yourself known to us through the healing and saving power of Jesus Christ, our Leader and Friend. Amen

PRAYER OF DEDICATION

Without the gifts of your Spirit, generous God, we would be unable to worship you by word and by work, but you enable our service as we are obedient to the prompting of the Spirit through Jesus Christ our Lord. Amen

PRAYERS OF INTERCESSION AND COMMEMORATION

Sovereign of sovereigns, bring to leadership and to authority those who honor your law and respect peoples of high degree and low degree, who respect minorities of racial, religious, and economic status. Promote justice that cannot be gainsaid and mercy that does not forget the victimized. Spare us from quick judgments that may prove unjust and irrevocable.

Bless your church with true mutual caring. Grant to the leaders of the church the trustworthiness that will encourage the suffering and the unhappy to call upon them for counsel and comfort in the name of the healing Christ. May our forgiving spirits readily receive those who are repenting of their sins and are in need of the assurance of pardon. May your church be a haven for the wounded, the sick, and the sorrowful. May we be at peace with one another and provide a community of serenity for those seeking tranquility and joy. Save our society from sexual predators that the innocent may not be ruined by their overtures and exploitation. Spare our aged from the scams of greedy and dishonest business operators. Bless all who seek to be good neighbors in helpfulness.

Bless all leaders in the world of sports, that genuine skill may be honestly rewarded and good examples be set for the young who look for role models among athletes.

May our young people find their heroes in many kinds

of activity: the arts, entertainment, education, business, government, the healing arts, cooperative enterprises, volunteering. Gracious God, call young and old to follow the example of Jesus of Nazareth, who went about doing good and healing the sick. We remember with thanksgiving all who have led us to Christ and who have been received into glory. Grant that in your appointed time we may also hear your "Well, done, good and faithful servant, enter into the joy of your Monarch." Amen

Proper 22 (October 2-8)

First Lesson - The writer introduces this epic poem of the testing of Job's faith by the adversary of God. Job 1:1; 2:1-10

Psalm 26

Second Lesson - The writer to the Hebrews declares the divine purpose in sending Jesus among us to raise us to the glorious dignity of the children of God. Hebrews 1:1-4; 2:5-12

Gospel - Jesus confirms that the original purpose of creation was that marriage is sacred and that divorce is one form of adultery. Mark 10:2-16

CALL TO WORSHIP

Leader: The grace of our Lord Jesus Christ be with you all.

People: And also with you.

Leader: Sing aloud a song of thanksgiving,

People: and tell all God's wondrous deeds.

Leader: Love the house in which we pray,
People: and the place where we give God glory.

INVOCATION

Universal God, every place where we address you is hallowed by our praise and thanksgiving inspired by the Spirit. Your Son blesses our homes as well as this sanctuary as he did the marriage at Cana in Galilee. Continue your blessed work among us for the sake of Jesus Christ our Savior. Amen

PRAYER OF CONFESSION

God unlimited, God self-limited, God extending our limits, surely you do not expect us to accept suffering without complaint! We are frustrated with illnesses that rage on, keeping us from doing the things that bring us satisfaction and recognition. Long nights and months of futility seem such a waste to us. Too often we question why it should happen to us, thinking ourselves to be better than others. We forget the exposure of your Son, Jesus, to all the circumstances of our mortality. We ignore the spiritual growth that could be ours in order to prepare us to minister to other sufferers. Forgive our resistance to the healing of spirit and body that your Spirit can enable through our faith in Jesus Christ. Amen

Declaration of Pardon

Pastor: Friends, hear the good news! In the Spirit Jesus still comes, healing those who suffer from various diseases

People: and freeing many who are captives of evil.

Pastor: Friends, believe the good news!

People: In Jesus Christ, we are forgiven.

[AND]

190

Exhortation

Bear your part in spreading the good news, whether in illness or health, weakness or strength, in the service of God.

PRAYER OF THE DAY

Synagogue-preacher, sick-bed-visitor, exorcist-of-evil, so teach us, so heal us, so clear us of evil, that we may be ready learners and teachers, visitors of the sick and the shut-in, of other sinners, gathering around you in one needy company. Amen

PRAYER OF THANKSGIVING

Creator of stars, nurse to the wounded, healer of broken spirits: that you have power to rule the cosmos fills us with awe. That you stoop to touch and heal us, fills us with amazement. You give new heart to the humble. We thank you for all that sustains life—human, vegetable, animal. Receive the thanksgiving of all creation, the psalms of your people, the music of the birds, the sounds of all living things. Hear us wherever we gather to praise you name. Amen

PRAYER OF DEDICATION

God of the gospel, we, along with pastors and elders, evangelists and teachers, healers and nurses, share the responsibility of spreading the good news, identifying with all sorts and conditions of people in order to communicate the word of your grace in Jesus Christ. Amen

PRAYERS OF INTERCESSION
AND COMMEMORATION

God for all nations, all cultures, all species, draw together all things in Christ, so that all creation and all humanity may learn to live in peace, all cultures are shared with appreciation, all natural resources are used with care for the benefit of the whole creation. Bless all who sit around tables negotiating disputes between superpowers, between labor and management, between spouses and families. Let reasonableness prevail and the widest viewpoints influence decision-making. Rebuke narrow-mindedness and nit-picking that prevent progress and justice.

Make your church an example of the breadth and length and depth of your understanding and love, not only through the connection of denominations in world councils of churches, but in the openness of any congregation to all the races that may live around it. God of compassion: in Jesus Christ you cared for all who were blind or deaf, disabled or slow to learn. Though all of us need help, give special attention to those who have handicaps. Show us how to be helpful so they may know we respect them for what they can do for themselves and for us. May we live together in your love. Hear our prayers today for those awaiting diagnosis of their illness, those who watch by the beds of the dying, those who are recovering from surgery, and all others. May the gospel of Christ bring hope to all who seek pardon for their sins and hope of everlasting life.

O God, our hope is in Jesus, who for a little while was made lower than the angels, but now is crowned with glory and honor because of his suffering and death, so that by your grace he might taste death for everyone and bring many brothers and sisters to glory. We are thankful for both our physical and spiritual kinfolk in heaven. By your Holy Spirit sanctify us also that we may be worthy to be received into your heavenly family, through Jesus Christ, to whom with you and the Holy Spirit be given all thanks and praise, time without end. Amen

Proper 23 (October 9-15)

First Lesson - When Job has a complaint against God, he does not know where to take it. Job 23:1-9, 16-17

Psalm 22:1-15

Second Lesson - Jesus is our high priestly advocate before the throne of God. Hebrews 4:12-16

Gospel - Jesus answers the basic question: "What must I do to inherit eternal life?" Mark 10:17-31

CALL TO WORSHIP

Leader: The grace of our Lord Jesus Christ be with you all.

People: And also with you.

Leader: Be satisfied with God's love when morning breaks.

People: We will sing for joy and be glad all our days.

INVOCATION

Awesome God, Incarnate God, Sovereign Spirit, we come to worship in the humble confidence your Spirit inspires as we are in the company of our advocate, Jesus Christ. Receive our hymns and prayers and instruct us through your spokesperson before us. We approach you through Jesus Christ our Lord. Amen

PRAYER OF CONFESSION

God of all possibilities, Gatekeeper of heaven, Assayer of Eternal values, you only are good. It is simpler to recite your commandments than to do them. Even if we do them, we often neglect the poor and risk eternal human values for the sake of perishable riches. Take from us all encumbrances that would prevent our entering the place of your rule. Apart from you, our salvation is impossible. Through Jesus, our high priest, we come expecting mercy and grace and timely help. Amen

Declaration of Pardon

Pastor: Friends, hear the good news! Jesus is our high priest, able to sympathize with us in our weakness.

People: Christ has been tested in every way like we are, but without sin. He intercedes for us at the throne of our gracious God.

Pastor: Friends, believe the good news!

People: In Jesus Christ, we are forgiven.

[AND]

Exhortation

Seek your happiness in the pursuit of wisdom and the acquiring of understanding. Wisdom is more profitable than silver and that gain is better than gold.

PRAYER OF THE DAY

Life's Gamemaster: we cannot hurdle all the expectations you have of us in order to win eternal life, so forgive our infractions of the rules and bring us to final victory with your needed help. Amen

PRAYER OF THANKSGIVING

God before all ages, God with all generations, God of the years to come, we are humbled by the thought of your eternal being. Your majesty inspires our praise. Your love moves us to sing and rejoice. The help of all good and delightful things sustains us in days of suffering. We trust you to lead us through the gate of wisdom, knowing that we can learn in days of suffering and gladness and years of testing and accomplishment. We will sing and be glad all our days, God of yesterday, today, and tomorrow. Amen

PRAYER OF DEDICATION

All-seeing and all-knowing God, we cannot hide our thoughts and purposes from you. Sift the motives in our worship and stewardship so that we may worship you more truly, through Jesus Christ our high priest. Amen

PRAYERS OF INTERCESSION AND COMMEMORATION

Not only can we find you in this house of prayer, eternal God, but wherever we are on any day of the week. You know our problems and will help us solve them. You know our lacks and how to meet our needs. Help us to depend on you day by day and call upon you for daily bread, as well as the Bread of Life for our souls.

When any of us or the whole congregation feel deserted in the time of suffering and trial, remind us of the resurrection of Jesus Christ that we may accept apparent abandonment as a momentary doubt and turn back with hope to commit ourselves and all we love to your providence. Give us patience in the face of opposition and ridicule, and strong faith in the face of doubters.

As Christ intercedes for us before your throne, we intercede also for the sinners among whom we live as well as for ourselves. May your Living Word, the Spirit, both convict us of sin and convince us of your forgiving and renewing grace. Amazing it is!

Renew our strength day by day and give healing and health to those absent from us because of illness or accident. May the Christ grant healing to our bodies as well as peace to our minds and hearts.

God eternal, Emmanuel, heavenly Spirit, guide us on our earthly pilgrimage that we may arrive at our heavenly home in peace. We rejoice in the communion of saints, our celestial connections in Christ and the community of the faithful who have preceded us. Hasten the day of our glad reunion when we will celebrate our total salvation together to the glory of your name, Paternal, Fraternal, Maternal God, One God forever. Amen

Proper 24 (October 16-22)

First Lesson - The majesty of creation puts the human critic in perspective. Job 38:1-7, (34-41)

Psalm 104:1-9, 24, 35c

Second Lesson - The writer to the Hebrews uses a mysterious priest as a forerunner of Jesus, the eternal priest. Hebrews 5:1-10

Gospel - Jesus explains that true greatness must be measured by the readiness to suffer for the good. Mark 10:35-45

CALL TO WORSHIP

Leader: The grace of our Lord Jesus Christ be with you all.

People: And also with you.

Leader: Set your love on God who answers when you call for help in the time of trouble.

People: We enjoy the fullness of salvation by the Most High.

INVOCATION

We set our love on you, O God, for you answer when we call for help in the time of trouble. As we hear your word and sing your praise may we enjoy the fullness of salvation by the Most High, through your lowly Son, Jesus Christ our Lord. Amen

Prayer of Confession

God of all life, we confess that we desire your will to be pleasure and prosperity. We have great difficulty accepting suffering as anything but evil, and we reject it as if it were beyond your power to redeem. Forgive our doubts and our unwillingness to serve you and others to the point of pain. In this we are unlike your Son and Mary's, Jesus Christ, who suffered with us and for us. Amen

Declaration of Pardon

Pastor: Friends, hear the good news! Jesus Christ was named high priest by God,

People: and being perfected in the school of suffering is the source of eternal salvation for all who obey him.

Pastor: Friends, believe the good news!

People: In Jesus Christ, we are forgiven.

[AND]

Exhortation

Seek true greatness through serving, not waiting to be served, but serving each other and all within your reach.

PRAYER OF THE DAY

Jesus Christ, person for others, grant us a portion of your Spirit that we may willingly serve others, whether we are honored or ignored, understood or rejected, loved or despised. We cannot accept the cup of suffering or the baptism of pain without your very present help. Amen

PRAYER OF THANKSGIVING

Active Listener, self-offering Priest, Spirit of prayer, we offer you our thanksgivings for the eternal salvation that is ours through obedience of faith in Christ, named our high priest forever. We are grateful for your patience with our ignorance and error and weakness, understood so well by Jesus, who gave up his life as a ransom for many. May our willingness to serve, rather than be served, be a further expression of our gratitude, most high, most humble, most loving God. Amen

PRAYER OF DEDICATION

Gracious God, if we have not received grace to give until it hurts, grant us the generosity to serve until it helps, so that you may be praised for our servanthood in the name of Jesus Christ. Amen

PRAYERS OF INTERCESSION
AND COMMEMORATION

Giver of the Spirit, Christ of the Spirit, Spirit of the Church, enliven your church everywhere that all of us who are baptized in the name of Jesus Christ may do the work for which you have called us with energy and conviction.

Grant wisdom to all who are called to lead local congregations, regional organizations of the church, national and international churches and councils of churches. May their concerted efforts bring healing to the sick, food and drink to the hungry and thirsty, clothing to the naked, visitation to prisoners, and the preaching of the good news to all who are captive.

Universal Spirit, draw together people of goodwill in all nations that they may discourage the forces of destruction and foster the rebuilding of what has been destroyed and the recovery of what has been laid waste.

Family Spirit, fill us with compassion that we may

befriend the friendless and sustain families who are taxed to the limits of their endurance in times of crisis.

Spirit of truth, inspire all who write and speak that they may be concerned not so much to be clever but to be honest and without deceit, enlightening all who share the responsibilities of the electorate, as well as elected and appointed officials who should serve us all.

Healing Spirit, bring peace of mind to the troubled, health of body to the sick, and wholeness to the spiritually broken, through Jesus Christ.

Eternal God, Jesus told us that you are God not of the dead, but of the living. In proof of his faith, you brought him back from the grave to give us all Easter assurance. As you were God for the patriarchs and matriarchs of Israel, so you are the God of our patriarchs and matriarchs in the church. We celebrate our unity with those who have proceeded us in the caravan of faith that leads to the celestial city. Guide us on our way that we may be reunited with all who have gone before us, through Jesus Christ who is the Way, the Truth, and the Life. Amen

Proper 25 (October 23-29)

First Lesson - Job's encounter with God leads to deep humility and a new chapter in the book of life. Job 42:1-6, 10-17

Psalm 34:1-8, (19-22)

Second Lesson - Jesus is exalted as the priest par excellence. Hebrews 7:23-28

Gospel - The loud and persistent cry of a blind beggar is not ignored by Jesus. Mark 10:46-52

CALL TO WORSHIP

Leader: The grace of our Lord Jesus Christ be with you all.

People: And also with you.

Leader: Rejoice and sing aloud for joy.

People: The Lord has done great things for us.

PRAYER OF INVOCATION

You have done great things for us, O God, so we come to you rejoicing and singing aloud for joy. Receive our praise and adoration with all our prayers, through Jesus Christ our Lord. Amen

PRAYER OF CONFESSION

Observant Parent, you know how we are. We can be moved by the sight of hunger without stopping our waste of food. We see the limitations of some of our energy sources but are slow to change our ways of using more than we need. We observe hazards and hurts in confrontation and conflict but are unwilling to learn the arts of conciliation. For our intransigence and intractability we pray for forgiveness, through your strong but docile Son, Jesus of Nazareth. Amen

Declaration of Pardon

Pastor: Friends, hear the good news! God has received Jesus Christ as our representative

People: bearing gifts and sacrifices for our sins.

Pastor: Friends, believe the good news!

People: In Jesus Christ, we are forgiven.

[AND]

Exhortation

Follow the priestly example of Jesus Christ and bear patiently with the ignorant and the erring.

PRAYER OF THE DAY

So that we may fittingly be called Christian, divine Light-Giver, grant us the vision to see where you go before us on life's road that we may follow you more closely and serve others with your insights. Amen

PRAYER OF THANKSGIVING

You are more than fair, good Lord, you are merciful. You are not stingy but magnanimous in your gifts of nature and grace. You are more than approachable: you are loving and outgoing. You are near us and with us and in all of your people everywhere. We do not love you enough, but we do love you, Person condescending, Person incoming, and may yet love you more. Amen

PRAYER OF DEDICATION

Creator of Eden and Paradise, plant in us the fruits of unselfishness after weeding out greed, through the living, giving Spirit of Jesus. Amen

PRAYERS OF INTERCESSION AND COMMEMORATION

Seeker and Savior of the lost, bless all who are looking for lost or kidnapped children. Encourage all who seek to expedite the search for missing children by printing pictures or by gathering information by whatever means.

Grant healing and help to all who use innocent children as pawns in family conflicts. Expedite the gathering of abusing parents, that in sharing their problems with one another under expert guidance, they may find the release that will bring to an end such unacceptable behavior.

Save us all from resorting to name-calling that may make us feel superior, but which does not enable understanding and reconciliation of people and parties of contrary opinions and hostile intentions.

Alleviate the frustrations of suppressed peoples that they may find more creative means of achieving change than hijackings and bombings. Sensitize governments in all parts of the world to the just needs of minorities that such frustrations may be dissipated through creative action. Defend us from those beyond the reach of reason and whose aggressions are solely for their own lust for power.

Bless those of our members and friends who are in the hospital, or are receiving treatment as outpatients. Grant human and divine support to those anticipating new kinds of treatment. Assist all healers that their work may benefit the sick.

Timeless God: By your power Jesus Christ was raised from death. Watch over the dying. Fill fading eyes with light to see beyond this life a home within your love, where pain is gone and all our frailties transfigured. Banish all fears. Let death come gently as nightfall, and faith give assurance of a promising day of glad reunion with Jesus Christ and those whom we have loved and lost awhile. May we hear in the solemn silence of death the joyful music of Easter in praise of our risen Lord. Amen

Proper 26 (October 30-November 5)

First Lesson - This is the beginning of the story of a Moabite woman who became an ancestor of King David and Jesus of Nazareth. Ruth 1:1-18

Psalm 146

Second Lesson - When Christ came as a high priest he entered the eternal Holy Place and offered himself not any animal sacrifice. Hebrews 9:11-14

Gospel - Jesus reemphasizes the two great commandments. Mark 12:28-34

CALL TO WORSHIP

Leader: The grace of our Lord Jesus Christ be with you all.

People: And also with you.

Leader: Fix your eyes on God's commandments.

People: We will praise God with sincerity as we learn of these decrees.

INVOCATION

God of order and love, may your Spirit surround us so that we are gathered in to consider your commandments, which are lovingly meant to prevent us from coming to harm and ruin. Encourage us to be honest in our confession of sin and need so that we may understand both your judgment and your mercy; through Jesus Christ our Lord. Amen

PRAYER OF CONFESSION

Good and great God, we come to you through Jesus Christ who intercedes for us sinners. We confess our sins, seeking forgiveness not only that we may be at peace with you, but also that we may pray for others. We are ashamed that our prayers are often as self-centered as our lives. Excuse our disordered priorities as we seek to change and reorder our lives according to the teaching and spirit of Jesus Christ your Son, our Lord. Amen

Declaration of Pardon

Pastor: Friends, hear the good news! God has chosen you to be saved through sanctification by the Spirit.

People: **We are saved by the Spirit through belief in the truth in Christ.**

Pastor: Friends, believe the good news!

People: **In Jesus Christ, we are forgiven.**

[AND]

Exhortation

To this he called you through the gospel, so that you may obtain the glory of our Lord Jesus Christ.

PRAYER OF THE DAY

Integrate our lives, One God, in an all-embracing love of which you are the center and from whose encompassing Spirit none are excluded whether near or far, through Jesus Christ your loving-to-the-point-of-suffering Son. Amen

PRAYER OF THANKSGIVING

Who can number the bounties of your goodness, Lord? You give us lands overflowing with milk and honey and seas alive with fish and growing things. Our skies shine with beauty and with power. The depths of the earth yield metals and energy sources in great variety. Our homes are visited by friends, and our neighbors help us in times of need. We have opportunities to learn together, to worship together, and to serve the common good together. We worship you with thankful hearts, with open minds, with willing hands, in the Spirit of Jesus Christ. Amen

PRAYER OF DEDICATION

Lord, save us from hypocrisy, not serving you with these offerings only, and ourselves with what remains in our keeping. Help us to use all our energies and all our means to serve you and our neighbors as ourselves: through Jesus Christ our Lord. Amen

PRAYERS OF INTERCESSION
AND COMMEMORATION

Covenant God, you keep faith forever. May we honor your great commandments as did Jesus of Nazareth and confess before the unbelieving that we are your people.

May your concerns be our concerns that we may seek justice for the oppressed and freedom for those who are denied freedom of thought and speech and prayer.

Bless all who seek to give food to the hungry through community pantries, refugee and catastrophe relief, agricultural self-help, fish farming, and animal husbandry.

Grant grace and wisdom to prison chaplains and all who counsel with prisoners before their return to freedom in our society.

We pray for those with surgical skills to open the eyes of the blind or sight impaired and all agencies who provide braille and recorded books to those who cannot see.

Minister to all who are bowed down, to the depressed and the addicted through healers and counselors, medical and spiritual.

Strengthen all who seek to make our society more caring and moral. As you love the righteous and watch over strangers and orphans and the bereaved, bless agencies that aid travelers and care for battered women and children. Restrain those who are violent and bring them into such caring custody that will restrain and pacify the hostile and agitated.

Grant health to all who are sick in body, mind, or spirit.

Risen and living Christ, we will not turn back from following you! Where you lead, we will follow; where you lodge, we will find our eternal home; your people shall be our people, and your Eternal Parent our Eternal Parent. Death may part us from our family and friends for a while but we look for the resurrection that brings us all into one heavenly family with you, Perfect Brother, and our Gracious Parent, with the Loving Spirit. Amen

All Saints
(November 1 or
First Sunday in November)

First Lesson - The prophet celebrates the conquest of death still to come. Isaiah 25:6-9

Psalm 24

Second Lesson - John foresees an immortality that is rich with a loving personal relationship with God. Revelation 21:1-6

Gospel - The death of Lazarus is the occasion for a miracle of Jesus and a promise of eternal life for all who would come after him. John 11:32-44

CALL TO WORSHIP

Leader: The grace of our Lord Jesus Christ be with you all.

People: And also with you.

Leader: God has spoken. Be glad and rejoice.

People: We will be glad and rejoice in the salvation of God.

INVOCATION

Eternal God, whose beginning is beyond our knowing, and whose life is unending, we come to worship because you have made yourself known to us in Jesus Christ. We are filled with wonder that in his incarnation he accepted mortality in order to provide for our immortality. We pray to you through his Living and Holy Spirit within us in the name of Jesus our Lord. Amen

PRAYER OF CONFESSION

Eternal God, nothing is more awesome for us than the death that we know to be inevitable, but which we cannot fully understand. We often question the timeliness of death, wondering if it is really occasioned by your plan or only the result of natural causes. Forgive any doubts that we may have that the resurrection of Jesus Christ does not hold promise for us and all your people as well. In his name we pray. Amen

Declaration of Pardon

Pastor: Friends, hear the good news! Grace and mercy are upon the chosen in Christ.

People: The faithful will abide with God in love.

Pastor: Friends, believe the good news!

People: In Jesus Christ, we are forgiven.

[AND]

Exhortation

Trust in God and you will understand all the truth you need on this side of the grave and have strong hope of eternity with God.

PRAYER OF THE DAY

Jesus, Lord of life and death, free us from the fears that bind us and help us to live a day at a time, trusting that you will provide for us what we need and in the end will take us to the place you have gone to prepare for us. Amen

PRAYER OF THANKSGIVING

God our savior, Christ our pioneer, Eternal Spirit, we give hearty thanks for our hope of life everlasting. Your prophets foresee banquets and other signs of your abounding grace. Your word promises the intimacy of personal caring and the wiping away of the last of our tears. Who can fully imagine the glories prepared by the Risen Christ for those who will be received through his grace? All glory be given to you the Alpha and the Omega, the Beginning and the End, the Creator of life and our final home. Amen

PRAYER OF DEDICATION

God invisible, God incarnate, God inspiring, the offerings we bring to our Lord's table are simple signs of our hope for the great feast you prepare in heaven. Receive these gifts and the offering of ourselves as living sacrifices acceptable to you through Jesus Christ our Lord. Amen

PRAYER OF INTERCESSION
AND COMMEMORATION

Abba, Father, your Son Jesus taught us to pray with such familiarity and also, most profoundly, to pray for the coming of your kingdom on earth.

Teach the rich the blessedness of generosity and the poor the enjoyment of what they have with thanksgiving and provide for them what they cannot live without. Teach us all to share unselfishly that there may be enough of your good gifts of the earth for all.

Grant to our leaders in government a concern for people that they may seek to provide for others the benefits they take for themselves. Teach us all to do to others as we would have them do to us.

Discipline our reactions to hostility so that our response to violence may be restrained and that both our private lives and our street lives may be more orderly and peaceful.

Bless every program that seeks to provide for the hungry both in emergency situations and where famine is endemic. May we share both surpluses of food and skills to help the hungry raise more food for themselves.

Be with your church everywhere, but especially we

remember Christian minorities that are persecuted for their faith by people and governments committed to another faith. Grant them consolations in their suffering and grace sufficient for their needs.

We rejoice in your promise that the holy ones of the Most High shall receive the kingdom and possess the kingdom forever and ever. We celebrate the communion of your people in heaven and on earth and hope for the day when your will may be done on earth as it is in heaven. Bring us all into one holy company, no longer separated from one another by any distance, or dimension, or disagreement that we may gathered to worship you, Father, Brother, Mother, in one holy family forever. Amen

Proper 27 (November 6-12)

First Lesson - The widow Ruth becomes a mother in a second marriage and a great-grandmother to King David. Ruth 3:1-5; 4:13-17

Psalm 127

Second Lesson - The role of Jesus as priest is described not only as the going in but the coming out again after the priestly offering is completed. Hebrews 9:24-28

Gospel - Mark contrasts the hypocrisy of the scribes with the sincerity of the poor widow in reporting the observations of Jesus. Mark 12:38-44

CALL TO WORSHIP

Leader: The grace of our Lord Jesus Christ be with you all.
People: And also with you.

Leader: Come to worship in simplicity and sincerity.

People: We vow to serve God in our daily life as we say our prayers in this company.

INVOCATION

This place is hallowed by our prayers, O God, and we come to this holy place to prepare ourselves to enter the sanctuary to which Christ has ascended as our high priest. The Holy Spirit inspires our prayers as we worship you in the name of Jesus Christ. Amen

PRAYER OF CONFESSION

Divine Provider, we confess that we sometimes doubt your provision for us. When we start scraping the bottom of the barrel, we cut back our sharing with others who have already run out and are hungry or in need. Forgive selfishness and independence that prevents interdependence and working together to solve distribution problems in the use of the resources of your good earth, through your compassionate Son, Jesus Christ. Amen

Declaration of Pardon

Pastor: Friends, hear the good news! Christ has entered into heaven.

People: Christ now appears in the presence of God on our behalf.

Pastor: Friends, believe the good news!

People: In Jesus Christ, we are forgiven.

[AND]

Exhortation

Just as it is appointed for us to die once and after that comes the judgment, so Christ having been offered once to bear the sins of many will appear a second time, not to deal with sin but to save those who are eagerly waiting for him. Encourage one another as you see the day drawing near.

PRAYER OF THE DAY

Save us, good Lord, from half-heartedness in our service of your church. Help us to find joy in the full use of all that we are and have in the saving name of Jesus Christ of Nazareth. Amen

PRAYER OF THANKSGIVING

Creator, Redeemer, Renewer, we give thanks for the fruitfulness of our vineyards and orchards, the productivity of our fields, and the reproduction of our cattle and poultry. We praise your name for sunshine and rain. We will give thanks also by our work, reclaiming overused lands, irrigating dry land, purifying polluted streams and lakes. We will be faithful managers of your lands and seas to the glory of your name and the benefit of generations still to be born. Amen

PRAYER OF DEDICATION

Holy God, what we give is nothing compared to the one-for-all, once-for-all sacrifice by Jesus of himself to put away our sins. Use our offering and witness to spread the good news of Jesus Christ, your Son and Savior of the world. Amen

PRAYERS OF INTERCESSION AND COMMEMORATION
(May be used prior to Election Day)

Most Sovereign God, most glorified Christ, most gracious Spirit, hear the prayers of your people, unworthy of an audience with you but grateful that you hear us in the name of Jesus. Guide and bless all in authority who look to you to pilot the ship of state. Show us who should be called out to lead us in local governments as well as in national elections. Help us to discern between impossible promises and achievable goals. Limit our hopes for human achievement with the knowledge that there is only one who is fully good, whose coming again we await.

Teacher of teachers, grant to all who teach, humility that is inspired by contemplation of the absolute wisdom that resides only in you. Free from presumption and dogmatism that there is nothing more that a teacher can learn from other teachers and even from the simplicity of the unlearned.

Carpenter Christ, call all who work to give themselves to workmanship in which they may find a deserved measure of pride of accomplishment. Save us all from shoddiness in half-thought plans and unfinished projects.

Healer of healers, grant patience to all who seek cures for human ills. Let concern for individuals as human beings pull together teams of healers that can meet the needs of persons in body, mind, and spirit.

Hear our prayers for those of our fellowship awaiting further surgery in the hospital.

Holy God, only Jesus Christ is worthy to enter your sanctuary not made by human hands, in heaven itself. We rejoice that he has appeared in your presence on behalf of us sinners. As our eternal high priest he has appeared once for all at the end of the age to remove sin by the sacrifice of himself. Graciously prepare us for death and after that the judgment, so that Christ, having been offered once to bear the sins of many, will appear to save those who are eagerly waiting for him. We depend on your promised grace and rejoice in the salvation of those already in your heavenly care and keeping. To you, Fatherly, Brotherly, Motherly God be ascribed all holiness, mercy, and peace, time without end. Amen

Proper 28 (November 13-19)

First Lesson - The barren Hannah rejoices in the son she promises to God's service. 1 Samuel 1:4-20
Psalm 16

OR

1 Samuel 2:1-10
Second Lesson - The writer of this letter describes the acceptance of Jesus as a prince of heaven after fulfilling his priestly office. Hebrews 10:11-18
Gospel - Jesus makes some awesome prophecies of events to come. Mark 13:1-8

CALL TO WORSHIP

Leader: The grace of our Lord Jesus Christ be with you all.

People: And also with you.

Leader: Let us proclaim how mighty are the deeds of God,

People: how glorious is the majesty of God's realm.

INVOCATION

God before all creation, Christ incarnate in our cosmos, Spirit re-creating what has been spoiled by the evil one, receive our worship in anticipation of heavenly reunion with the Christ risen and ascended to glory. Hear our prayers for his sake. Amen

PRAYER OF CONFESSION

Glorious God, Divine Human, Eternal Spirit, we get so mired in the stuff of every day that we rarely see visions and dream dreams. We are busy about daily routines for making a living and so preoccupied with the immediate that we do not look for signs of your judgment nor the changing seasons of divine history. Forgive our sins and wicked deeds for the sake of Christ's offering for our sins once for all. Amen

Declaration of Pardon

Pastor: Friends, hear the good news! Christ offered for all time one sacrifice for sins, and took his seat at the right hand of God.

People: Christ offered for all time one sacrifice for our sins and took his seat at the right hand of God to intercede for us.

Pastor: Friends, believe the good news!

People: In Jesus Christ, we are forgiven.

[AND]

Exhortation

Be alert and wakeful, for you do not know when the head of the human household will return to take account of our stewardship of the earth.

PRAYER OF THE DAY

Offspring of time and eternity, in monotonous times as well as in times of personal and communal crises, remind us of the limits of time so that the breaking in again of the eternal will not catch us unaware. Amen

PRAYER OF THANKSGIVING

Ancient in years, Offspring of time and eternity, timeless One, we are grateful for the moments in time when we are given a glimpse of eternity—when the poignancy of poetry or story give us full appreciation of love; when the coming together of people achieves fulfillment of true community;

when a high moment of music or other living art gives us a vision of ageless beauty; when a prophetic word or action discloses the vision of truth. Be worshiped, O God, now and ever. Amen

PRAYER OF DEDICATION

True God, there are offerings for sin no longer, for by the offering of Christ have all been consecrated. What we offer then is what is being perfected for all time by that climactic sacrifice of Jesus Christ. Amen

PRAYER OF INTERCESSION
AND COMMEMORATION

God of Israel, Lord of the church, Eternal Spirit, the offerings at the temple are succeeded by the offering of our Lord Jesus on the cross. Bless your church as it surrounds the banquet table of our Lord and receives the bread and cup, which signify his self-offering once for all as the means of grace for our salvation and everlasting life. Bring to this congregation those who should be received by baptism and confession of faith that there may be a growing communion of believers and disciples of Jesus Christ. Maintain your church with a faithful ministry of pastors gladly given by their parents not to fame and fortune, but to humility and faithful proclamation of your word and sincere priestliness in prayer and the offering of the sacraments.

Save us from false messiahs who would lead us astray, taken captive by their egotism and cleverness in self-promotion. Keep the innocent from the grasp of such proselytizers and grant freedom to those already in their hands.

Bless all who are called to marry and establish a family. Comfort the childless and the infertile and guide those with medical skills to overcome their emptiness. Save us from thoughtless abuse of the means of procreation. Teach us to value all life, the children of the poor as well as the rich, the promising and the disadvantaged.

Heavenly Householder, we celebrate the eternal home in the heavens, not made with hands. Your Son has gone to prepare a place for us and we pray that we may be made fit spiritually for communion with you and those who have gone before us. Hear our prayers now and always in the name of your beloved Son, Jesus. Amen

Christ the King - Proper 29 (November 20-26)

First Lesson - The final words of King David are full of hope for the future. 2 Samuel 23:1-7

Psalm 132:1-12, (13-18)

Second Lesson - Not a kingdom of military power but a kingdom of priests is envisioned by John on Patmos. Revelation 1:4b-8

Gospel - The ruler of the realm of the Spirit defends himself before a ruler of this evil world. John 18:33-37

CALL TO WORSHIP

Leader: The grace of our Lord Jesus Christ be with you all.

People: And also with you.

Leader: Holiness is the beauty of God's temple while time shall last.

People: We worship God in the sanctity and freedom from our sins, which Christ gives us through his life's blood.

INVOCATION

You are holy, God, our heavenly Parent. You are holy, Jesus, our heavenly/earthly Brother. You are holy, Spirit of God in the Church. As we worship you, consecrate us by your purifying Spirit that we may become your holy children. Amen

PRAYER OF CONFESSION

Ancient in years, Firstborn from the dead, timeless Spirit, we confess that too often we are overawed by the wealth and power of human rulers, forgetting that they are as mortal as we are, and that only Jesus Christ has won an impressive victory over death. Forgive us if political and national loyalties have superseded the dignity you offer us as a royal house of priests to serve you. You have sent us your faithful Son Jesus Christ, but we listen to him less attentively than to less demanding voices around us. We admit that we too are among the people whose sins have wounded him. Forgive and free us from all our sins by the giving of his life's blood. Amen

Declaration of Pardon

Pastor: Friends, hear the good news! The Christ loves us and freed us from our sins with his life's blood.

People: The Christ makes us a royal house to serve as priests of his God and Father.

Pastor: Friends, believe the good news!

People: In Jesus Christ, we are forgiven.

[AND]

Exhortation

Look for the one who is coming with the clouds! Call to repentance all who have offended him.

PRAYER OF THE DAY

Sovereign of all, who is and who was, and who is to come, raise us above the tides of natural events, and the ebb and flow of history, so that we may glimpse the glory of your eternal realm, and be satisfied with no lesser honor than to serve you as witness to the truth in the company of Jesus Christ. Amen

PRAYER OF THANKSGIVING

Your majesty, eternal God, precedes and exceeds the grandeur of the seas, and your throne, unlike the passing dynasties of nations, does not pass away. Your truth, Sovereign over all earthly rulers, is full of grace and peace and not full of empty threatening so typical of the tyrants of our world. We join with the Seven Spirits before your throne in extolling you, the Alpha and the Omega, who is and who was and who is to come. May our thanksgiving continue not only while we have life and breath, but through such coming generations as shall live until all people and nations of every language shall serve you. Amen

PRAYER OF DEDICATION

Our greatest gifts, Sovereign Creator, may not be given with pride, because none can be worthy of your majesty. Receive them as token tributes to you signifying our humble service in the royal priesthood of all believers, through Jesus Christ, our Princely Priest. Amen

PRAYERS OF INTERCESSION
AND COMMEMORATION
(May be used for the Sunday before Thanksgiving)

God of all continents, as we celebrate thanksgiving again this week in our land of plenty, we pray for those who live in lands of drought and famine. Bless all who are undertaking to feed these starving people. Grant speed and safety to all who fly the big cargo planes laden with food raised by the farmers of our fertile lands. As we pray for the success of the emergency feeding program we remember also the need for long-term solutions to the problems of hunger on every continent. Break down the barriers of indifference that allow the people who have enough to ignore the plight of those who, out of sight, are out of mind. Inspire scientists in the exploration of problems of drought and the need for local solutions to land use and productivity. Help us to utilize new cosmic views from space to solve such problems, as we get new perspectives on our global village.

We pray for Peace Corps volunteers and agricultural missionaries who have gone to share knowledge and experience with less developed countries and peoples. Give them skill in teaching and demonstrating the practices that have improved our diets and health in this bountiful country. While enjoying the bounty and variety of the harvest, teach us to avoid waste that we may have more to share with others in need anywhere in the world.

Hear our prayers for family and friends who are sick, anxious about uncertain diagnoses, impatient for a cure, longing for relief from pain. Bless us all whatever the nature of our need. Comfort those who are dying.

You are the Alpha and the Omega, O God, who is and who was and who is to come. Our hope is in you because of Jesus Christ, the faithful Witness, the Firstborn of the dead, and the Ruler of the kings of the earth. He loves us and frees us from our sins by his blood and makes us to be a kingdom, priests serving you. We are grateful for those known and dear to us who already serve before your throne. May your grace and peace enable us to serve you here until you call us to higher service. To you, God and Father of our Lord Jesus Christ, and to the Son and to the Holy Spirit be glory and dominion forever and ever. Amen

Scripture Index